fixing the **money thing**

fixing the
money thing

Gary Keesee

 Please note that Destiny Image's publishing style capitalizes certain pronouns in Scripture that refer to the Father, Son, and Holy Spirit, and may differ from some publishers' styles. Take note that the name satan and related names are not capitalized. We choose not to acknowledge him, even to the point of violating grammatical rules.

DESTINY IMAGE® PUBLISHERS, INC.

P.O. Box 310, Shippensburg, PA 17257-0310
"Speaking to the Purposes of God for This Generation and for the Generations to Come."

This book and all other Destiny Image, Revival Press, MercyPlace, Fresh Bread, Destiny Image Fiction, and Treasure House books are available at Christian bookstores and distributors worldwide.

For a U.S. bookstore nearest you, call 1-800-722-6774.
For more information on foreign distributors, call 717-532-3040.
Or reach us on the Internet: www.destinyimage.com

Trade Paper ISBN 13: 978-0-7684-3684-6
Hardcover ISBN 13: 978-0-7684-3687-7
Large Print ISBN13: 978-0-7684-3688-4
Ebook ISBN 13: 978-0-7684-9025-1

For Worldwide Distribution, Printed in the U.S.A.

15 / 19 18

endorsements

Dave and I have always stressed the importance of excellence and integrity in the area of finances. In a day and age where debt and financial stress are crippling American families, it is vital that we understand God's plan for our finances. I believe the practical, everyday insight Gary shares will educate and empower you to take control of your finances and discover the peace and financial freedom God desires for you.

—Joyce Meyer
Best-selling Author and Bible teacher

Pastor Gary has touched a nerve in the Kingdom of God with his amazing book *Fixing the Money Thing.* His fresh and bold revelation and presentation regarding finances and the Kingdom of God leads the reader to the point of a life altering decision...Do I believe what I've always believed and do what I've always done therefore achieving the same results I've always achieved; or...do I trust God and take Him at His word and open up a door to my God given destiny?

This book has forever altered my thinking regarding money and the Kingdom of God! I highly recommend it to anyone needing new direction and blessing in finances.

—Tom Davis
President and Founder
Amber Rose Ministries
HealingPackage.com

The Greatest gap in the world is between what we know and what we apply that we know. This book illustrates "How to" apply God's financial principles, not another volume on man's ideas, written for everyone who has been trusting in everything, but God's unfailing Kingdom precepts. Learn "How to" fix the money thing so you can be free to pursue your destiny in Him.

—Dr. Dean Radtke
Founder and CEO
The Ministry Institute

Most financial resources are tedious, hard to understand, and frankly boring. At least that's what I thought until I found "Fixing the Money Thing" by Gary Keesee. I'm not a money expert, and that's why I use "Fixing the Money Thing" like a textbook. My copy is dog-eared, underlined, and marked-up. My wife and I have discussed it, argued about it, and thanked God for it. It's readable, easy to follow, and best of all, brilliant. Whether you're a financial novice or an expert, this book will change your thinking about your financial future. Too many people wait until it's too late to solve their money problems (if ever). But now, you have someone in your corner that can change everything. Buy the book, and watch your bank account turn around for good.

—Phil Cooke,
Media Consultant and author of *Jolt!*

table of

contents

THE FIX

FINDING MONEY

fixing the **money thing**

the disaster

introduction

why i wrote **this book**

If you're looking for a financial advisor with alphabet soup trailing behind his name (you know, MBA, CPA, CFP, XYZ!), then the pages that follow may not hold the kind of advice you're looking for. But if you're interested in hearing from a guy who, after doing pretty much everything wrong and finding himself at the brink of bankruptcy, discovered that God had a lot to say about finances and stepped into a whole new life of financial freedom by applying God's principles—well, I'm your guy.

I suspect you wouldn't have picked up a book titled *Fixing the Money Thing* if your money thing didn't need some fixing. And the fact is, I have been right where you are (or worse!) financially. I have known both the pain of owing people I couldn't pay and the joy of total freedom from debt. And I know exactly how I got free, with God's help, from that stressful life of despair to a life of freedom and purpose.

Since then I've spoken to tens of thousands of families and hundreds of thousands of people in the United States and internationally about fixing their money thing. I have helped people in just about every conceivable financial situation. And I have helped people realize that they usually already had the power and resources to become debt free—they just lacked knowledge. In fact, I love taking people down that road to freedom because I have great compassion for anyone who is trapped in the bondage of debt. Like I said: been there, done that.

Before you jump to conclusions thinking that I must be some kind of super brain and you could never hope to understand the financial strategies I'm going to present in this book, let me assure you that I didn't get the best possible start in adult life. If you had known me back in high school, you wouldn't have voted me most likely to set the business world on fire. Back then I considered education little more than a necessary evil. My teachers knew me as the kid who never talked. I was shy and extremely uncomfortable around people. Tests were just an opportunity to rebel. I frequently turned them in without bothering to answer a single question. Believe it or not, the 1.3 GPA I left high school with was probably better than I deserved.

On the pages that follow, I'll share some of the most valuable things I learned while I lived in financial prison. I will unveil the Kingdom principles that the Lord taught me. And I will share my own mistakes freely because my heart grieves for those who are going through many of the same financial struggles I endured. I hate it when I see so many American families being damaged and even destroyed by financial stress. It is my life's passion to help people fix the money thing in their lives, so they can truly embrace the life and the purposes God has destined for them.

Don't allow yourself to feel condemned about your current situation as you read this book. This is a book of hope. It's about answers. Of course, a book of this length can't provide specific prescriptions for every possible problem, but it can bring you principles and solutions for the most common mistakes. The only book with *all* the answers concerning life is the Bible. But it is my hope that in this book you'll find practical encouragement for your situation in life—financially and spiritually. Wherever you find yourself, take comfort in knowing that it is never too late for a personal financial revolution. It is never too late to dream exciting dreams, and to envision a future full of passion. No matter what shape your finances are in today, it is never too late to see yourself living debt free. It is possible.

Through my true-life stories and suggested exercises, I will share some powerful keys and insights about finances. I will show you where the money that creates financial freedom comes from as well.

Take comfort, and know that you won't be making this journey alone or bearing this responsibility totally by yourself. I will be walking it out with you and, of course, God will help you realize this dream of freedom because it is His dream for you too.

I want you to think of the thoughts and ideas you'll find on the following pages as fragments—pieces of financial wisdom that, though they're usually right before our eyes, are frequently overlooked. These "scraps" of wisdom might not seem significant by themselves, but when added together with other "scraps" of knowledge, they can form the basis for a real breakthrough where your finances are concerned.

Jesus knew the value of "scraps." He fed 5,000 men and their families who had followed Him far out into the countryside in their hunger for spiritual food. He showed the power of increase in God's Kingdom when He took the only food available to them—five loaves of bread and two fish—and gave thanks for them. Right before the eyes of His skeptical disciples, the bread and fish multiplied again and again.

But the multiplication of the bread and fish was not the entire story. There was something the disciples didn't initially see or understand—the power of *the fragment*. The power of the fragment is what this book is about. The power of the fragment is where you'll find your answer.

And although the financial fragments I'm referring to may currently seem hidden to you, they've probably been in plain sight all along. Jesus made reference to the principle of the fragment in John 6:12-13:

> *When they had all had enough to eat, He said to His disciples, "Gather the pieces* [the fragments] *that are left over. Let nothing be wasted." So they gathered them and filled twelve baskets with the pieces* [fragments] *of the five barley loaves left over by those who had eaten.*

Again, those fragments were overlooked by the disciples! Jesus had to tell them that they were of value and worth picking up. And when they did follow the Lord's direction, the payoff was astounding—they had many times more food in *fragments* than they had to begin with. There was abundance to be had in the fragments!

So it is with you and me. You already have the resources to be free. You just need to find and pick up the financial "fragments" that are almost certainly scattered all around your life. I suspect your current income is enough to resolve your debt problem—including getting rid of your mortgage—in five to seven years! The fragments are there for the gathering. It is my privilege to walk beside you and remind you of the value Jesus placed on gathering them.

My hope is that you'll find the reading of this book an adventure unlike any you've ever traveled. Along the way you may just realize that there are hidden treasures amid your financial clutter.

I'll show you what God thinks of money and how He wants you to uncover what's already yours.

Today that shy, backward boy who graduated from high school with a 1.3 GPA has come to fully experience life and the joys of the Kingdom of God. I own three companies that produce millions of dollars a year in gross revenue. My wife Drenda and I have a nationally televised weekly show, "Faith Life Now." We travel the world teaching pastors and their church members the financial principles of God's Kingdom, and we also pastor a growing and dynamic church. In our spare time we're parents to five children, three horses, five cats, three dogs, and a ferret.

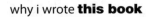

Trust me, life at the Keesee home is *very* busy. I could never have enjoyed these blessings and many others had I not discovered and learned the principles of financial freedom. These practical truths and strategies I now excitedly share with you in hopes that you too will experience the good life. After all, God designed you to live a life of purpose and abundance.

chapter 1

our **story**

If I'm truly going to help you, I believe it's important you understand this road I've traveled—the one that took the Keesee family from a lifestyle of financial stress and crisis to one of peace and purpose. My financial freedom did not come as a result of one major revelation, but rather it was comprised of all the lessons I learned along my journey, the lessons I learned on the road. It's important you know how truly messed up I was and how far down God had to reach to pull me up to ground level. You need to appreciate how powerful God's Kingdom principles of finance are.

Those years of struggle were filled with some pretty intense feelings of failure and constant, bone-crushing stress. But as painful as it was at the time, I now know it laid the groundwork for my life's destiny and fired me with a passion to help others avoid the financial holes I fell into. In the same way, it's important for you to remember as we begin this journey to financial deliverance that the successes you enjoy will be about more than just money. Even more important, you'll gain a better understanding of your relationship with God's Kingdom and your place in it.

As I mentioned in the Introduction, school was not high on my list of priorities as a teenager. As a matter of fact, my GPA was so low I ranked second in my class…second from the bottom that is. We're talking some serious underachieving here.

Then something happened that completely changed the trajectory of my life. At the age of 18, I gave my heart to Jesus and began a journey of radical transformation. As anyone who knew me back then will confirm, it was a life-changing event in the truest sense of the word.

Later that year a non-Christian friend of mine was throwing a birthday party for me at his house along with a few other non-Christian friends. They had prepared a birthday cake for me along with some great grilled steaks. I remember all of us sitting down at the table to eat. As I cut my first bite of steak—had it on my fork, on the way to my mouth—all of a sudden something happened to me that I had never experienced before.

The Holy Spirit fell in that place (at least to me) and stopped me in midair. I literally froze. The presence of the Lord was so strong, I really couldn't move. My fork just hung in midair as I wondered what I should do. I looked across the table, and my friends were staring at me, wondering what was going on.

I remember mumbling something like, "Uh, could I please be excused for a few moments?" Right behind me, luckily, was the screen door that led out to the backyard. I remember kind of standing up and stumbling out that door wondering, *What is this feeling?* I knew it was the Lord, but I had never experienced it before.

As I walked out into the backyard, suddenly the presence of the Lord became even stronger. I fell to the ground, and as I did I saw a picture in my mind—not an outward vision—but a picture of myself standing up, holding a Bible in my hand, and preaching or teaching to people sitting in folding chairs.

Then a voice said, three times, "I have called you to preach My Word. I have called you to preach My Word. I have called you to preach My Word." After that, the presence of the Lord lifted just as suddenly as it had come. I don't have to tell you, I was shaken.

As I made my way back into the house, my friends stared at me for an explanation of my strange behavior. I simply said, "I'm not sure what happened just then, but I think I was called to preach." More staring followed my announcement.

Understandably, they didn't know what that meant or what to think of it.

I knew, however, that what I had experienced was the real deal. For me, the shyest kid in my high school, to be called to preach—it had to be God. Up to that point, my greatest ambition had been to have a cabin in the woods of Alaska where I could enjoy nature and generally be left alone. Suddenly I found myself being prompted by the Holy Spirit to pursue college. College! For Mr. 1.3 GPA? Although I felt confused and uncertain, the Lord kept confirming in my heart the need to go to college and, not surprisingly, He directed my steps to make it happen.

At that point I had already taken a few courses at a nearby Bible college and, as evidence that I really was a new man, I earned an A in each class. Imagine that—second-to-last in my graduating class and here I was receiving As at Bible college.

When I worked up the nerve to start the application process at a major four-year college in Tulsa, Oklahoma, I included my record in these classes, along with my embarrassing high school transcript. My hope was that they would see the sharp contrast between the two and realize something had changed in my life. That was pretty much what happened.

I got a call from a person in admissions who said, "Mr. Keesee, we see that your grade average in high school and your SAT scores do not meet our minimum grade average requirements. But it looks like something changed for you after high school. Could you please tell us why you took those Bible college classes and why your results were so much better?"

Of course, that gave me an opening to explain that I had become born again and that I was very much a different person than the one who barely drug himself through high school. I was asked a few more questions about my future plans and my reasons for wanting to attend that university. Finally, at the end of the conversation, I heard, "Mr. Keesee, we will be accepting your application."

I remember packing my tiny, rusted-out Fiat with nervous excitement and driving it all the way to Tulsa. I was a college man!

My first year there was definitely challenging. Though I was growing, my study habits and work ethic were not yet strong. I was the guy with no vision, but God was changing that too. I remember my freshman English class. One of our first assignments was to write a paper—just the type of thing I consistently blew off in high school. I'll never forget when I received it back from the teacher, on the front page in big red letters was written the letter F, and under the letter were these words: "Is it possible you even went to high school?"

After that rocky start, I quickly caught up on what I should have learned in high school and got better as I went along.

Step by step, milestone by milestone, my life's direction changed in those college years. And toward the end came what would turn out to be the greatest blessing of all. I was introduced to a classmate named Drenda.

She was gorgeous, and she had talent. The funny thing is she was voted "Most Likely to Succeed" out of a class of 550, and she had a 4.0 average in high school. She led every extracurricular activity she could get her hands on. Little did she realize that she was marrying someone at exactly the opposite pole of life.

God put us together, and she was the greatest help in my life—to help me believe in myself, and to help me believe that I could win. She was my cheerleader. Although it was frustrating for her, many, many times she would cheer me on.

We borrowed money to get married. And that mistake set the tone for the early years of our marriage. The fact is, it put us on a slippery downhill slope in our finances for years.

My first job was selling life insurance and other investment products. The job was "straight commission," meaning I only got paid when I sold something. Needless to say, this wasn't the best situation for someone who cringed at the thought of meeting new people—"cold-calling" as they termed it—basically phoning or visiting total strangers and trying to sell them something. Anxiety became a constant in my life. And so did financial pressure.

For years my spotty performance had us living "hand-to-mouth." That meant turning to debt every time we had too much month left at the end of our money. Of course, each time we charged or borrowed we fully intended to quickly repay, but those intentions rarely got translated into actions. As a result we fell further and further behind.

Eventually we had maxed out ten credit cards, had three finance company loans at a whopping 28 percent APR, owed back taxes of more than $13,000, owed relatives more than $26,000, held a home mortgage, owed more on two rusted-out cars than they were worth, and had judgments and liens filed against us. Financially, life was a complicated mess.

The stress created by these obligations was huge.

One memory in particular remains painfully fresh to this day. Yet it was typical of those dark days. I had one credit card left that hadn't been cancelled by the lender, and it was maxed out (or very close to it). With my family in tow, I went to the local gas station praying all the while that the card would clear so I could buy both gas for my car and dinner for my family. Dinner, by the way, was going to consist of those questionable sandwiches you find in mini-marts, tightly wrapped in saran wrap and sealed with a sticker. Sad to think, but McDonald's was even out of our price range at that point.

I pumped my gas, grabbed some sandwiches, and then held my breath as the cashier swiped my card. I watched for the approval code to appear. (*Please work, please work, please, please.*) After what seemed like 15 minutes, "APPROVED" flashed across the LED screen. I exhaled, snagged the bag of sandwiches, and hit the exit, afraid the Visa computer might suddenly change its mind before I could get out the door.

In my relief and hurry, I jumped into my car and sped off, only to feel a sharp jolt as the gas pump handle and hose—the handle and hose still stuck in my open gas tank—were ripped from the pump.

The feeling of failure at that moment was unlike anything I had ever felt. The look of despair and disappointment in Drenda's eyes, the confusion on the faces of my children, and the stares of the gawking bystanders combined to create a searing sense of humiliation I didn't think I'd ever get over.

I was desperate in those days, and we experienced financial stress almost on a daily basis. I want to relate a few more examples of how we lived in those days so, if you're in a desperate situation, you will have hope that you too can change.

One especially bad example came at a time when I'd scraped together enough money to open a new checking account at the branch office near a farmhouse we had recently rented. Because I was frequently in the bank putting out little financial fires, I'd gotten to know the manager, who usually handled my transactions. On several occasions I took the opportunity to share my faith in Jesus Christ with her and tell her about the blessing such a relationship brings. I even had one of those Christian logos printed on my checks.

But one time, a commission check I had been expecting didn't arrive as hoped. True to form, I'd already written checks against it and I was up a creek. By the way, necessity isn't the mother of invention. *Desperation* is. And my desperation led me to a series of increasingly dicey maneuvers designed to cover one insufficient check with another.

I'll never forget the morning the phone rang, and it was the bank manager's voice. I recognized it immediately. She said, "Mr. Keesee, we know what you're doing, and you need to stop. I need a check in my office today for the full $2,000 you have been floating. We're going to close your account, and you never can do business in our bank again."

Wow, that'll wake you up!

With this brilliant mind of mine, I'd come up with the idea of going down the street to another bank and opening a new checking account. Then I would write a (bad) check from that new account and deposit it into my regular checking account, and then cover it the next day with an equally bad check from the regular account to the new checking account.

Back and forth each day, I would cover a bad check with a bad check—expecting that I would only have to keep it up for a day or two. It actually lasted for two weeks, and the amount was $2,000. One day the system just didn't work. The banks caught on, and that's when my phone rang.

I had to walk into the bank and apologize to my branch manager, the same one I'd been talking to about how great God was. I told her, "Don't hold this against God. He had nothing to do with it. It was only my doing."

As I said, those were dark days. My home at the time was barely livable. Let me tell you, living in an 1850s farmhouse sounds charming on paper. But most of that charm is lost when you have no money to do something about its broken windows, cracked window frames (complete with weeds poking through the cracks), non-existent closets, and single bathroom, which doubled as a utility room that all seven of us had to share.

Our cars were in the same shape—bent frames, rusted out floorboards, and mileage topping 200,000 on each. Literally everything around us was falling apart and I had to look my precious wife in the eye and tell her we were trusting in the Lord for our future.

The town we lived in was mostly farmland, but developers were buying up the land and building big, beautiful homes near our little farmhouse. Every year the city hosted a Parade of Homes where the latest décor and appliances were shown off by various builders. I tried to avoid going there for a few years fearing that my wife would find her little farmhouse all the more oppressive. As a new year came around, again my wife asked if we could go down and look at the homes.

I was paralyzed. I knew if she went down there and looked, without a doubt, she'd want one.

I hedged and stalled about it but finally gave in and took her there. I remember we were walking from house to house together when at one point I turned and found she wasn't beside me anymore. I looked around and about 30 feet behind me, I saw her standing on the sidewalk with tears streaming down her face.

She looked up at me and said these words, which still hurt to this day, "When can I have a house?"

I didn't have an answer. I didn't have a clue. I was simply trying to survive. I was just working on keeping us going one more day. Pawn shops were a way of life. We were unable to fill our cars with gas. We bought everything at garage sales. The carpet on my kids' bedroom floor had literally been retrieved from a trash bin. Their bed mattresses were from a nursing home. Everything we had was used. Very used.

Although we were Christians, we apparently were missing something somewhere. Everything came to a head when, at a point when we were totally out of money and the creditors were calling, an attorney called one morning and said, "Mr. Keesee, we're filing suit against you for $1,900. You have three days to get this money to us or the suit will be filed."

We had reached the end of our rope. We had borrowed from everyone we could borrow from. Every credit card and every credit option we had was declined and cancelled. On top of all that, I had been sick for several months and unable to work, which caused my business income to dry up.

Life was beyond tough. And it had me asking a pointed question: *Where's God?*

I can remember the day I collapsed on my bed in desperation to pray. In response to this desperate plea, the Lord brought Philippians 4:19 to mind. It says, *"And my God will meet all your needs according to His glorious riches in Christ Jesus."* It was clear to me that my needs were not being met. Yet God's Word clearly stated that they should and would be met. For the first time, I began to think that maybe the failure to see this promise fulfilled was my fault, not God's.

There's something missing, I thought. *There's something I need to understand about God's Kingdom for things to operate as He promised.* I continued to pray, and the Lord spoke. "Gary," He said, "you trust in debt and the world's system of finance more than you do in my Word."

It hurt to admit it, but it was true. I realized that, up to this point, if I needed something and didn't have the money, I'd just borrow it—"trusting God" to help me eventually pay it off. God, however, was telling me there was a better way. There was a new system He wanted me to trust in rather than the old, failed system of credit, debt, and misplaced hope. He wanted me to learn how His Kingdom operates so I could live a life of freedom and abundance. All this information came to me in just a few moments of prayer.

Filled with a fresh hope, I hurried downstairs to Drenda and repented to her for how I badly I'd missed the mark as the head of the house. I hadn't been living or leading according to the ways of God's Kingdom. To this day I can still remember where we stood when we prayed simply and honestly from our hearts: "Father, we don't understand Your Kingdom. We can't get ourselves out of debt. We're in a mess, but we're going to trust Your system. We're going to find out how it works, and if we fail at it, we fail at it, but whatever the case, we're not going to use debt anymore. We're going to find out how Your Kingdom operates."

We purposed in our hearts then and there to find out how things operated in God's domain, and we got serious about studying and applying God's Word.

We certainly had plenty of motivation. We had to have answers because things were crashing around us and now with this latest lawsuit threat, we knew that time was up.

The next day I went about my business as usual, making sales calls at customers' homes well into the evening. As I was leaving my last appointment for the day, I shook my client's hand and turned to leave. I made a deliberate point of shaking hands and saying my goodbyes *inside* their homes so that they wouldn't walk outside to see the dilapidated old heap of a car their "financial advisor" was driving. I was sure they'd think, *If he's so smart about money, why isn't he driving a nicer car?*

Much to my alarm, my client followed me to the car and watched as my old rattletrap filled his driveway with billows of white smoke when I turned the key in the ignition. He was a mechanic by trade and he quickly diagnosed my trouble—water in the oil and a busted head gasket. His instructions were simple: drive the car no further than home and then on to the auto repair shop tomorrow, absolutely not an extra mile more. Now, for someone with a little money lying around to spend on car repairs, this would have been unwelcome but manageable news. But I wasn't such a someone. I wasn't about to run up a repair bill I couldn't possibly pay.

I prayed aloud as I drove home, throwing my fears and worries at the feet of the Lord. "Father, how am I going to fix this car? I can't sell it broken. I can't afford to fix it. I still owe the bank money for it and I still owe the attorney, plus other bills," I pleaded. "Lord, I really don't know what to do. It would almost be better if the car just burned up and the insurance took care of it."

As I pulled into my office, I noticed a bubble on the hood of my car and I also thought I smelled fire. Then suddenly, the bubble burst into flames and the flames engulfed the front of my car within minutes. The fire department arrived just in time to hose down the charred heap of scrap metal that moments before had been my car.

I was stunned and thrilled all at the same time.

I fumbled around for words and finally said, "Lord, when I said it would be better if the car burned up, I didn't really know you were *listening.* I certainly never really believed it would happen!"

But it had. And, since the car was totaled, a check from the insurance company was delivered the next day. That settlement check took care of my pending debts to the attorney, the balance owed on the car, a few smaller debts, and yes, even some groceries for my family. In all my years of driving, that has been the only car that caught on fire, and it happened just as I said out loud that statement in prayer.

Drenda and I were still beginners and we had a lot to learn, but we had started learning to trust in God's system of provision for us. As we did, we saw blessing after blessing. One of the first was the gift of a very used but reliable station wagon that someone gave us to replace the car that burned up. More provision followed as God consistently honored our commitment to pay off all the debt we had accumulated in decades of spending beyond our means. One night the Lord gave me a dream about starting a business, which I still own. As I was faithful with that vision, money began to come in and our lives were changed.

In just two-and-a-half years we went from being slaves to debt to being free people as we paid it all off. From there, we began saving for the future, and we put back $100,000 in just three years. We began paying cash for every service we employed and everything we bought. I can't tell you how great it felt to walk into a car dealership and pay cash for a car. We paid cash for our 55 acres of land on which we planned to build our dream home, and we paid for half of the 7,700 square foot house with cash as well.

We have since paid the house off, but I can remember the day we broke ground. Drenda and I stood there and watched as the basement was being dug and we just literally cried and shook. We couldn't believe what we were seeing, and the emotion of it all was hard to handle. The basement of our new home had *more* square footage than the entire farmhouse we were moving from. It had only been a few short years since we were broke and almost bankrupt. We knew without a doubt that what we were seeing was a direct result of the Kingdom of God and our decision to learn and apply its laws.

Throughout this process, God faithfully walked alongside us, gently teaching us His principles as they relate to His Kingdom.

We now believe this truth with all that is in us: Everyone can win in life financially and everyone can get out of debt, no matter how deep a hole they've dug. It's who they are following and whose system they are operating under that makes all the difference in the world.

My friend, if God did it for us, He'll do it for you. Today is the day to change your future. If you'll apply the basic financial principles and strategies I'm about to share, you'll find real freedom and true purpose for your life.

Let's get to it.

chapter 2

the joneses' **scary** little **secret**

Over the last 19 years, Drenda and I have been living a dream—a dream the Lord gave me to help people get out of debt. It was a call to step out by faith and start a company that would minister to husbands, wives, and entire families to help them bring their finances into order and see the blessing of operating in God's economy. The result of our obedience has blessed us beyond measure. It has exceeded our wildest dreams as we've reached out to over 100,000 families, literally, across their kitchen tables and helped them to realize that relief from the pressures of debt and the blessings of abundance from the Lord were theirs just for the asking.

One day in prayer, the Lord said to me, "My people are like the people of Israel were—trapped and enslaved in Egypt, but I want My people free." He brought to mind Proverbs 22:7, which says, *"The rich rule over the poor, and the borrower is servant to the lender."* I gave further thought to the life of what we traditionally think of as a slave. Visions of overworked, underpaid people came to mind.

My mind immediately went to the images from history books or movies that most of us associate with the word *slavery.* I envisioned relentless slave drivers always pushing for more work from their already beaten-down work force. Whether it was the Roman Empire or the days before the Emancipation Proclamation in America, workers would slave away 12 to 14 hours a day, often in dangerous conditions, with just a little food and shelter as payment. Time off? They were at the mercy of the boss. And they attended their retirement party in a pine box.

This doesn't seem too far removed from the way many people are living today as they toil away in the typical American job.

One time my kids and I were driving in Columbus, Ohio, where we live and found ourselves caught in a huge rush-hour traffic jam. We've always been entrepreneurs, working from our own home and meeting with clients in the evening, so my children had not experienced the typical 5 P.M. freeway gridlock. This particular day was unusually heavy, and as we drove in towards the outer belt surrounding Columbus, one of the children said, "Daddy, what's happened? Maybe there's been an accident."

"No," I said. "There hasn't been an accident. This is how most people live every day. In fact, this happens twice a day." Well, my children were shocked. One said, "Daddy, this is horrible. Why would someone want to do this twice a day?" I said, "They don't really want to, but they have to. This is how they live."

And then I told them, "Don't worry. I'm going to train you to be an entrepreneur, to set your own hours, to have freedom. Most people do not have that; they're simply slaves." Of course, I knew what it felt like to be a slave with no options, and I wasn't going to train my kids for that kind of future. I wasn't going back either. I found out that I liked freedom. No, let me rephrase that, I loved freedom!

So how did we get out of that system of slavery?

The details of how Drenda and I found freedom from debt by operating under God's Kingdom principles will emerge as we go along. As they do, I'll lead you from wherever you are to the freedom that is available to you as you put your life, your resources, your possessions—your everything—under the authority of Jesus Christ. It won't be quick. It won't be completely painless. It won't come without sacrifice. It *will,* however, produce the most freedom and peace of mind you've experienced—second only to making Jesus the Lord of your life.

You, my friend, are in for a change for the better.

Let me tell you up front—if your benchmark for success is matching your friends and neighbors purchase for purchase on cars, electronics, vacations, clothes, and other high-ticket items, you're not alone. It's how most of America lives today. But remember this before you "one up" your neighbors with the biggest riding lawn mower on the block: the bankruptcy courts are full of Joneses, Smiths, and Johnsons.

If you're keeping up with the Joneses, I have news for you. I've been to their house and I've looked at their spreadsheet. I've seen their finances top to bottom and, believe me, the Joneses are headed for a financial cliff. You don't want to follow them, much less keep up with them.

Today, Americans live in homes they can't afford, drive cars they haven't paid for, sleep on beds they've purchased through finance companies, and wear clothes bought on a maxed-out credit card. Keeping up with the Joneses has practically become an American pastime. It's created a nation of spenders who want the right house, the right car, the right television, and the right mobile phone. And they want it right now.

A 2006 *New York Times* report said, "Americans are awash in red ink. Consumer indebtedness is soaring, the savings rate is down to zero and people are filing for bankruptcy at record rates."[1] Bankruptcies jumped 30 percent in 2009 alone to over 1.4 million compared to the number of filings in 2008.[2] The catch that many fail to recognize is, as one financial Website put it:

> ...you may be trying to keep up with the Joneses while the Joneses may be trying to keep up with other Joneses, and so on, and so on, and so on. The Joneses may be struggling financially too, a lot more than you might think.[3]

This endless keeping up is a lose-lose situation for all involved claims Juliet Schor in *The Overspent American*. "We are impoverishing ourselves," she writes, "in pursuit of a consumption goal that is inherently unachievable."[4] Think about it. Would anyone in their right mind go after something they could never, ever achieve? What's more, this endless cycle brings with it side effects that can harm your physical health and your emotional well-being and compromise your walk with the Lord. And that's just you! To make things worse, this free-spending lifestyle almost always brings with it fallout for others—including verbal abuse, neglect, and even abandonment of spouses and innocent children. Nice, huh?

Sure, many people are aware that in their drive to keep up appearances, they are living above their means. Others, however, know their finances are not what they should be, but they have no idea just how deeply in debt they really are. In my initial visits with struggling families throughout the years, I've seen that most underestimate the negative gap between their monthly income and their spending by at least $300 to $400, and those are the ones who are at least making an effort to keep some kind of financial books.

Just how unaware are some people? One case that stands out in my mind is that of a man I'll call "Bill." Always faithful to work hard, bring home a respectable paycheck, and turn it over to his wife, Bill was stunned and red-faced when his only credit card was rejected for a minor purchase. "Th-th-that's impossible," he stammered, "I just gave my wife my paycheck last week to pay bills."

Unable to ignore the electronic denial, the clerk returned the card to Bill. Convinced there had been some sort of mistake with his credit card, Bill returned home and questioned his wife about how something like that could happen. Before she could get more than a few words out, she began crying. She then went to the bedroom, pulled out a hidden shoebox, and handed over the statements of 43 different revolving lines of credit. Each one offered cash advances, very low introductory interest rates, and larger and larger amounts of available credit.

Having been short of funds to meet their monthly expenses at one point in the past, she simply took advantage of one of the numerous credit card offers that regularly hit their mailbox. One cash advance met the need for the time being. That is, until it came time to pay the advance back...with high interest...and late fees...and other hidden penalties. Not surprisingly, another credit card arrived within days, offering yet another cash advance.

What ensued was a robbing Peter to pay Paul scenario that continued for years until she couldn't keep the deception going any longer. It was a literal house of cards. Credit cards. And when it collapsed she couldn't make the payment on the card her husband carried. The deception and sense of betrayal brought Bill's marriage to an end. But his is not an isolated case. It's estimated that up to 80 percent of the divorces in our country are due, at least in part, to financial strains and pressures—strains that exist because couples are trying to live way above their means.

Believe it or not, Bill's wife and her collection of 43 credit cards doesn't hold the record among the many people I've counseled over the last 19 years. That sad honor is held by a woman who, I'm sorry to say, never did come to know the sweet victory of financial freedom. Though she reached out for help by calling me to come and assess her situation, in the end, she was unwilling to change her out-of-control spending habits. When I sat down with her, she listed credit card after credit card and kept going and going until I ran out of room on my data sheet. I had to turn the sheet over and keep going.

All totaled, she had 52 cards in varying states of use—maxed out, delinquent, or both. Fifty-two. That's a full deck if she was playing cards.

But the game she was playing wasn't solitaire. It was high stakes poker with her future, and she was losing it.

Knowing I was treading on raw, emotional ground, I began as gently as I could in my appeal to her. "Ma'am, the first thing we have to talk about is your allegiance to this system of debt. The only way to get out of debt is to stop using debt. We need to cut these credit cards up and devise another way for you to live," I suggested to her.

With that, she burst into tears and hung her head in shame. "How will I be able to live?" she cried. "How can I buy medicine? How will I ever be able to buy shoes again?"

How can I buy shoes? ***Shoes?!?***

It's a shame, but it was thoughts and questions just like those that had put her deep in debt. And without a significant change of thinking and attitude, it was only going to get worse. If only she could see that she was trading peace of mind for a pair of the latest shoes.

Here's another example. In this case, reckless spending brought more than a rejected bank card or the threat of wearing outdated shoes.

For this financially naïve young man, a constant stream of unsolicited credit card offers was too much to turn down. So he didn't. And the more offers he accepted, the more he got. In his mind, riding this rolling snowball of credit down the hill was fun. And each offer felt like a further validation of his credit-worthy status.

This insanity—both his and that of the banks that kept sending the offers—allowed him to take a four-year world tour without a job, living on cash advances from the cards that kept coming. During the trip, he met his future wife. She thought he was a wealthy American businessman. They married and lived for two years in London while he maintained the image of being a successful businessman, but all the while he was living on the cash advances. Running out of credit card options and now with the first baby being born, he was afraid of telling his wife the truth about the lie he was living.

When at last the gravy train of cash advances was finally tapped out, he resorted to forging his brother's name to keep the snowball rolling a little longer. The snowball hit a wall in the form of a knock on the door. Two FBI agents wanted to chat. Following his formal indictment, he was sentenced to a significant time behind bars.

The silver lining in his story is that during his imprisonment, both he and his wife came to know Jesus as their personal Savior. Some time after his release, this gentleman heard me on a radio talk show and called me, insisting that I come by that night and hear his story. I visited him at his home, and he gave me a sketchy outline of a story the likes of which I'd never heard before. Without any prior knowledge about his background, no one would ever suspect this average-looking father of four was a convicted felon, guilty of stealing on a grand scale. He was so incredibly normal. So...regular. He was the neighbor who you'd talk football with over the mailbox. The one whose kids would get your mail and newspapers when you were out of town.

This regular guy has a message for you. He wants his experience to serve as a strong warning to people on the edge of financial ruin. Before I left his home, he begged me to caution others about the pit he fell into. "Gary, as you travel the country and teach people about money and debt, please tell them this: I ***never*** intended to ring up over $220,000 in credit card debt. Would you ***please*** tell people to be very, very, very careful using a Visa card?" Or any other credit card, I would add. I promised him I would, and by putting his story in this book I am keeping that promise.

Besides underestimating just how much debt they have, most Americans are also asleep at the wheel when it comes to "saving for a rainy day" or even for a cloudy and overcast one. According to a survey by Bankrate.com:

> Fewer than four out of ten American adults have an emergency fund to fall back on in the event of some financial disaster...Consequently, a costly emergency, such as an unexpected unemployment or major medical expenses, could send unprepared adults into a financial tailspin that could lead to years of debt or even bankruptcy.[5]

Most experts recommend having an emergency fund of six months of living expenses readily available. However, even savings to cover 90 days would prevent many unexpected expenses from becoming full-blown financial disasters that take years to recover from.

It's hard to believe, but one simple medical emergency can be the first domino in a sequence that ends in foreclosure on your home or a bankruptcy filing. I see it all the time. I see it with people who think it can't happen to them—good, honest people who work hard for the dollars they bring in but can't seem to get around to saving a few for emergencies. And an emergency always comes to each of us eventually. These good people always plan to get around to saving someday.

In what I think can best be described as an "identity crisis," Americans are using their purchases to paint the picture of how they wish things were in their lives, not as they truly are. Again in *The Overspent American,* author Schor describes this mentality as being "absurd and sad...We are, after all, a nation of accomplished spenders, slaves to advertising, and status symbolism. The conspicuous fruits of our consumption shout out our aspirations and insecurities."[6]

I'd like to bring some statistics to your attention, my friend, in hopes of instilling in you an awareness of the seriousness of the time in which we live. You see, we Americans, being an optimistic bunch, tend to think things will always go on as usual. But I've worked in the financial field for 29 years, and even in that period of time, things have not gone on as usual. In fact, things have continued to deteriorate, and this on-going financial crisis has only continued to escalate.

When I first started this business, we used to quote an alarming statistic in our seminars which revealed that in 1984 the average family spent 86% of their disposable income. Of course with consumer spending that high, much of it was funded by debt..That number was outrageous and we used it to illustrate to people the danger of over spending and using debt.

But by the 1990s, that number had risen to 95 percent.[7] So in my seminars I began pointing out the huge change that had happened in ten years in our country as far as consumer spending went.

In 2002 I had to revise my presentation as the debt load that Americans were carrying was getting out of hand and becoming dangerous. The following chart will show the explosive growth of debt that was taking place in the country relative to disposable income.

Outstanding Consumer Debt as a Percentage of Disposable Income

1975	62%
1980	69.5%
1985	73%
1990	84%
1995	90%
2000	97%
2005	128%

Source: Board of Governors of the Federal Reserve System, Flows of Funds Accounts of the United States, Historical Series and Annual Flows and Outstandings, Fourth Quarter 2005 (March 9, 2006). Available at http://www.federalreserve.gov/releases/Z1/Current/.

Well, I've obviously learned to write that statistic in pencil. Robert Manning reports on the Web site creditcardnation.com, "that today the average American household's indebtedness, as measured by the share of household disposable income, has marched inexorably upward from the 86% in 1989 to more than 140% today, according to the economic Policy Institute's State of Working America."[8]

However, with the recent financial turmoil and millions of dollars being wiped out from housing markets and 401(k) plans, the savings rate is starting to go back up in 2010 as families scramble for security.

There are other statistics we can look at that will help us understand the cultural trends driving the typical family's financial health. For example, bankruptcies over the last few years have risen to an all-time high of 1.6 million, a rate that consistently keeps rising.[9] You've probably heard a lot of talk in the news about the "sub-prime mortgage loan crisis." The rates of foreclosures were already at record-high levels when they soared another 79 percent in 2007. That rate increased during 2008, with the April 23rd edition of *The Wall Street Journal* reporting that 7,500 homes were being foreclosed on a day.[10]

According to HousingPredictor.com on May 13, 2010, they predicted 16.5 million foreclosures in the United States by 2015 and stated that 7.3 million have occurred in the last two years since the crisis began.[11]

It's no wonder people are defaulting on their mortgages. According to information gleaned from FreeMoneyFinance.Com, 90 percent of families buy things they can't afford. In fact, 80 percent of graduating college seniors already have credit card debt, and 19 percent of bankruptcy filings in 2002 were college students.[12]

Forty-nine percent of average American families don't have enough in savings to cover even one month's living expenses should they suddenly lose their income. MSN Money tell us that the average family has about $87,881 in total debt which may or may not sound high but that is the average.[13] This number takes on greater significance when you find that the average household also spends $1.22 for every dollar earned.[14] Again, that's the average. The families I've seen and worked with had much higher average numbers, typically $20,000 to 30,000 or higher for credit card debt. Some had consumer debt upward of $50,000 to

60,000 counting car loans. And you have to remember that any average figures include the minority of people who actually have savings and minimal debt. These folks tend to bring the average down.

Speaking of averages—the average personal wealth of a typical 50-year-old American, according to Moneyrelationship.com, including home equity, is less than $50,000.[15]

I know these statistics are alarming, but this is what I have seen for 19 years and that's why I use the strong term *slavery* to describe the life of the average American.

What a sad description to have to apply to anyone. But it's doubly sad when it accurately describes believers—a group that has such a great covenant of provision and wisdom available to them. Unfortunately, over the years it's become hard to tell the difference between a believer and someone who doesn't know the Lord, at least financially speaking. I believe there are many reasons for this, but the bottom line is that there should be a difference. Overall, I believe the Church has not leaned on the principles that are in the Bible. Instead, people have adapted to the financial culture and have, as a result, incurred the same financial bondage that the world enjoys.

Sadly, I see it all the time, and I could cite numerous examples that I've seen over the years. But I want to cite two examples that will help you get a clear picture of what I'm talking about. The first involved a young, single mother whom Drenda and I found crying at the altar one Sunday morning at the church we had attended. The tears flowed as she told us how she felt moved to give to the church's building fund but couldn't afford to do so. We quietly handed her a $100 bill and told her that she now had money to give, which she, in turn, gave toward that offering.

A few weeks later, we stopped by that same church to pick up something. As I was walking into the church, I couldn't help but spot a brand-new, shiny, red convertible equipped with all the bells and whistles. It was so new that it still had the temporary license tags on it. I entered the church and saw this same woman cleaning the front hallway. After I greeted her, I asked her who owned the impressive new car, not even imagining that it could be hers. She looked at me with a proud smile and said, "It's my car." My face must have had a shocked look on it because without me saying another word she said, "God told me to get that car." Next, as if reading my mind, she was quick to explain, "Don't worry, though. I didn't buy it; I just leased it!" Still in shock, I asked her how much the payment was and she then looked down and said $500 a month.

Why would a person do something so stupid? I think the answer is easy to understand.

She was a single mother and things were tough. This car offered her an escape from reality, a new identity. In simple words, it made her feel better about herself. Debt clouds a believer's true identity, an identity that first and foremost should be rooted in who we are in Jesus Christ. But debt, in subtle and not-so-subtle ways (as in the case of the red convertible) allows us to live a lie, to pretend to be someone we're not, to live in ways we can't afford. We stop being authentic. The purchasing power, which in the beginning is so exhilarating, carries stout consequences.

Just ask the couple I counseled who had come to me describing their financial status as "desperate." They weren't exaggerating. In fact, after reviewing their statements and other financial records, I realized it was an understatement.

When I left our first meeting, I told them I'd return in a week with a plan to help get them back on firm financial ground. When I did return, imagine my surprise when they proudly showed off the brand new Cadillac they'd purchased since my last visit. Shocked, I had to ask what prompted this major purchase. "Why? Why? Why?" I asked, "When we're in the midst of negotiations and counseling and trying to get you out of debt, why did you go and buy a new car?"

In a somewhat awkward, pathetic tone they began to explain. "Well, we figured that once we made a commitment to get out of debt, we wouldn't ever go into debt again," began the husband. "And since we realized that the car we had was too old to last as long as it would take us to get out of debt *and* save to pay cash for another one, we decided we'd better get it *before* we committed to getting out of debt."

That's sort of like an obese person stocking the refrigerator with ice cream the night before the big diet is scheduled to start. And even if they really did need a new car they failed to realize that a good used one would have been better. Again, I believe the issue wasn't the car but the status the car offered them. The $600 monthly payment, however, was now a hindrance to their financial freedom and stood in direct opposition to their goal of being debt free.

Stories like this are common, and advertisers know how to sell to our identity and emotions while we ignore our utility and function.

I was stunned by a statistic I read in the Business Section of my own hometown paper, *The Columbus Dispatch*. The headline read: "Debt Is People's Biggest Worry...Finance Problems Rank Higher Than Terrorism and Disasters."

The article said:

> Americans are more worried about their growing personal debt than they are about becoming victims of a terrorist attack or natural disaster. More than 80% of Americans say that debt from credit cards, car loans, student loans and so-called "payday loans" are a serious problem. And 35 percent say their level of debt has increased in the past five years.[16]

But the following statistic from the same article is what really caught my attention. It reveals that 23 percent of Americans are not able to pay even their minimum debt payments. Well, I knew what that would mean. If they can't pay their minimum payment, they're headed for bankruptcy. The article then went on to say that 49 percent of American families cannot pay off the amount of debt they charged the previous month, meaning that basically one-half of the American population is increasing their debt burden every single month.

The problem, the survey said, is so pervasive that it's becoming a growing threat to the American middle class and to the American dream. In fact, for families, the amount of consumer debt in our culture has doubled in the last five years.

USA Today carried this sad headline: "Many Marriages Today Are 'Til Debt Do Us Part.'" In the article, we learn:

> Couples who married in recent years have a 40-50 percent chance of divorcing or separating during their lifetime. How often is money an issue in these divorces? Nearly 40 percent of financial planners who have worked with these kinds of couples say it's frequently a key factor.[17]

Things are getting rough out there. After talking to one of my clients in Colorado by phone a while back, she sent me this e-mail:

> I wanted to give you an update of what has been happening since your call. The next morning after we talked, the front page headlines of *The Rocky Mountain News* read: "Foreclosures eclipse record with numbers of 17,782 homes in the Denver metro area; 25,421 homes in outlying affluent areas; 3,754 and 8,352 in surrounding areas; and 18,784 homes in the city of Grand Junction, all in foreclosure."[18]

These homes represent real lives and the collapse and loss of millions of dollars. These same kind of statistics are found all across the United States and serve as a warning to the irresponsible debt lifestyle that most Americans live. Sadly, the segment of our society in which debt problems are rising the fastest are retirees. For example, a *USA Today*, (January 23, 2007) headline read: "Retirees Up Against Debt." The article goes on to say that 70+ year-old retired adults are the group in which debt is growing the fastest. The second fastest-growing segment in debt is 50+ year-olds.[19] This is truly another disturbing fact of our debt-ridden culture.

Over the years, Drenda and I have been in homes and have ministered to thousands of families and have seen all kinds of financial dysfunction. One of the saddest things we've ever seen came the day we were asked to go to a new client's home. Drenda and I had been busy and we wanted to spend some time with each other, so she came along on the consultation.

At that time, we were still living in our little old farmhouse, and it was kind of discouraging sometimes to see where we were at in comparison to others. As we pulled into the client's driveway, we were shocked to find that we were pulling up to a huge mansion. In the driveway were expensive sports cars, and we thought to ourselves, *Why are we here? Why have they called us? They can't have any financial problems.*

As we walked into the house, I noticed there wasn't any furniture. The marble floors were beautiful, and the woodwork was absolutely gorgeous, but the house itself seemed sterile and empty.

We sat down at the kitchen table and began to talk to the couple. As we did, the young mother began to cry. We learned they had a mortgage of over $800,000 and all kinds of debt on top of that. They were struggling just to survive, and this beautiful home they had recently built had become a nightmare. It had not become a home; it was simply a house.

They were so strapped that they said they hadn't even been able to give any money to their church in tithes. They knew that was wrong, and that's not how they wanted to live. We counseled them, took the information, and I advised them above all to sell that house.

After I had talked with them, I ran across the husband several months later. He thanked me, and let me know that they had, in fact, sold their house, which released them from a lot of unnecessary pressure. Finances can put a squeeze on life that, without help, can cause us to lose sight of life itself.

I remember another couple that told me they were serious about getting out of debt "this time." So serious, they told me, that they had "frozen" their credit cards. I took this to mean they had called the bank and cancelled their cards. *Good for you,* I thought. But then they went to their freezer and pulled out a bowl of frozen water with several credit cards suspended inside. The problem, I told them, was that there was also a microwave in the house.

Cancelling the cards would have meant cancelling the false security they felt in knowing those cards were really still available. They hadn't burned the bridge behind them. They'd just made it a little inconvenient to access.

In each of these cases, seemingly small decisions led people down a path to financial ruin. No one plans to destroy themselves financially, but subtly and slowly the deception of debt weaves its web until it's too late for escape. The good news is that there is escape available to you if you have the courage to make the decisions that lead to freedom. If you find yourself currently enslaved with financial problems, unpaid bills, or even threats of foreclosure—don't be discouraged. I'll walk you through the process that has helped thousands of families find financial freedom.

But before I do, it's vital that you recognize that this crazy race to keep up with the Joneses is just that—crazy. I need you to stop basing your identity in your stuff and in your status. You will find out that freedom is really the most rewarding thing in life. Nothing can replace the feeling of having freedom and having options. Nothing.

chapter 3

how to **lose money**

People with money know something that those without it don't: When Visa and other such creditors induce people to live beyond their means and spend what they don't have, creditors stand to benefit in a big way and get lots of money from those people for a very, very long period of time.

This may be best shown by how aggressively retailers, especially major department stores and "big box" stores (think Target, Wal-Mart, Home Depot), push their branded credit cards. Their financial directors have come to realize that more often than not, they stand to make more money from lending money (in the form of interest on credit card balances) than they do off the actual sale of their products. Their offer of a one-time discount of 10 to 20 percent for your first-time credit purchases at the cash register can quickly turn into a big payday for them—and all they have to do is take a slightly lower profit margin than they originally planned on that first purchase.

"Macy's, Sears, JC Penney and all their friends in the retail industry know how to lure us in for the big catch," says Michael Abramowitz of

Bankrate.com, "They offer a sweeter deal for our purchases if we'll sign up for a harmless department store credit card."[1]

It all comes down to who has the money at any given point in time. If you've got the dollars, you're in the clear. If not, any one of several hundred retailers who can borrow at the low rate of 5 to 7 percent would gladly *loan* you the money at a rate of 20 to 36 percent by having you use their credit card.

Now, this explains why you and I are constantly bombarded with credit card offers. I'm amazed at the way I continually get credit card offers in the mail by the dozens week after week—many, surprisingly, from the very same company!

In other words, I'll get a card offer one day from a certain bank, and then a couple of days later, the same offer from the same bank. And so it goes, over and over. Why? How can they afford to do that? Aren't they aware that I didn't respond to their offer the first time they sent it to me? Are they thinking that I didn't read it or that it got lost in the mail?

Oh, no, not at all. They're just playing a numbers and timing game. They're fishing. They're waiting patiently for a moment in time when pressure will cause you to think twice about their offer. By constantly dangling a baited hook in front of you, they're ready to catch you at your moment of weakness. Exactly what are they catching? Let me give you an example.

The fact is they know from experience that you're worth waiting for. One yes from you is worth all the money they spent while you said no. I'll show you why.

Let's assume that you have $1,000 in a savings account earning 6 percent, and it stays in that account from age 20 to age 65. During that 45-year period of time, it would grow at the 6 percent rate to over $13,000. Now, that same $1,000, earning a 21 percent department store credit card rate would grow to over $5 million. That's right. Just $1,000 left in an account for that same period of time, which equals 45 years, would grow to $5 million.

Now, growing at a finance company rate of 28 percent, that same money grows to $67 million! We always need to remember that the odds overwhelmingly favor the house in the credit card game. That's why more than 4.2 billion credit card offers were mailed out to Americans last year.

It's also easy to see why Americans are losing thousands and thousands of dollars to credit cards. The modern-day money changers are definitely changing money, but it's not in your favor.

What lenders at all levels seem to understand is the **Rule of 72**. With the Rule of 72, you can quickly figure out how long it will take for the lender to double their money. In this case, we're talking about the amount of money you have borrowed. No big surprise—the higher the interest rate, the quicker the payback. To do the actual math, divide 72 by the interest rate you are currently paying on any type of loan and that's how long it will take for the money to double. In other words, that's how long it takes you to pay back *twice* what you originally spent on goods and services. If you've signed on for a department store card at an astronomical 24 percent rate, it would only be three years (72 divided by 24 = 3) before you actually paid *double* for whatever it was that you had to have, but didn't actually have the money for at the time.

Besides charging us high interest rates, credit cards also have the tendency to cause us to spend more than if we were actually spending the dollar bills. Most studies indicate consumers spend 12 to 18 percent more if they're paying with plastic rather than "real money." There's just something about actually removing the dollars from your wallet and giving them to the sales person, a very visible transferring of wealth, that makes us give second thought to whatever we're buying.

Beyond bringing in additional sales, credit cards also bring in thousands and thousands of dollars through various fees. Fees for using your card too much. Fees for extended inactivity. Fees for sending in your payment late. Fees that are written in complex and confusing legal talk and printed in type smaller than a phone book. "The fine print is a license to steal, rigged to trap the unwary with huge fees and rate increases. Know your enemy," warns Peter Davidson of Bankrate.com. Davidson continues:

> ...credit card companies have managed to stack the deck in their favor, thanks to obliging lawmakers and regulators who have allowed them to gouge consumers for exorbitant fees and unconscionable interest rates.[2]

Thankfully Congress did pass the Credit Card Accountability, Responsibility, and Disclosure Act of 2009, which went into effect on February 22, 2010. This law made some major changes to the fees that credit card companies can charge the consumer. Some of the most important changes that went into effect involved making the **universal default penalty** illegal. This penalty allowed a lender to raise interest rates for any and all reasons. A lender would many times raise a person's interest rates if they were late paying another credit card. For instance, a payment received two days past due to Sears would have enabled all of your credit card issuers that use the universal default tactic (as stated in the legal double-talk of the user's agreement) to begin charging you an increased interest rate. The new law also stopped over-the-limit fees unless the card holder opted in on those fees. In other words, in the past a credit card company would go ahead and pay a charge that took a person's balance over the limit and then attach an over-limit fee to the monthly statement. The new law does not allow a lender to charge over-the-limit fees unless the consumer has stated they indeed want the company to pay over-limit transactions and are aware of the fees involved. There were other limitations of fees in the new law that helped the consumer, but the danger of the credit card to the financial well-being of the typical American family has not been minimized.

Most people do not understand the significance of what may be considered a small fee. But be informed. There's big money in small fees, especially over a long period of time.

In my financial practice, I had a client who discovered an old life insurance policy in the attic when his parents died. The policy was on the life of his father. The unusual thing about this policy is that it had been purchased by his grandparents back when his father was born. The monthly premium had only been $1.72, but it had been paid for over 70 years.

At first glance, that $1.72 monthly payment seems insignificant, and yet if you were to make this same investment for 70 years at 14 percent interest (what the banks and insurance companies will loan it out at on Visa Cards), you would have almost $3 million. Yet the policy only had a cash value of $500 and a death benefit of $1,000 to show for 70 years of spending. You see, the insurance company knew something that most of us don't: the time value of money and the Rule of 72.

The lenders, or the money changers, don't want you to realize the value in a dollar here or a dollar there, a subscription fee or monthly membership here or there. You may see it as just a few dollars, but to banks and credit card companies these monthly fees and small amounts add up to millions of dollars each year from individuals just like yourself.

Besides attracting traditional customers, the money changers have increased their barrage of seemingly free money to all segments of our culture. College students, even without jobs, have become a major source of new customers. The money lenders hope to snag these older teenagers and 20-somethings early and keep their hooks in them right through all the start-up expenses in their new professional lives—including wardrobes, first apartments, weddings, and beyond.

The average credit card debt of recent college graduates today is more than $2,300. To understand the impact of this debt, consider this: a new graduate with a balance of $2,300 who is making only the minimum payments each month could get married and have a 10-year-old kid before paying off the balance he was carrying. All totaled, the $2,300 starting balance would take 10.9 years to pay off and would end up costing more than $4,200.[3]

Today, it seems everyone is receiving unsolicited credit card offers. "Debt is being pushed and pushed and pushed on people," says Lauren Saunders of the National Consumer Law Center.[4] Statistics from Smart-Money.com seem to prove this as they cite that 1.5 billion credit cards are in use in the United States, an average of almost five per person.[5] Access and availability to use our cards is no problem either, as 24 million merchants across the world accept credit cards and account for 2.5 trillion credit card transactions a year.[6]

Now can you see why they're so intent on getting new customers and enabling irresponsible spending habits? There's big, big money in credit cards. Remember what I said earlier about the odds always favoring the house where credit cards are concerned.

Let's go back to 1950 and find out exactly how this all came about.

The first credit card was called the Diner's Club and came into existence in that year. It was created by a man named Frank McNamara. Finishing a meal in a New York restaurant, he decided it would be convenient if there was a way to pay for the meals without using cash. He developed a pasteboard card with a list of 27 restaurants that accepted it on the back. The first plastic card came out in 1955. Today, there are roughly 20,000 different credit cards now available in the United States.[7]

By the way, the record for the most credit cards held belongs to Walter Cavanaugh of Santa Clara, California, who currently has 1,497 credit cards that are active, with a $1.7 million line of credit. He has a certain type of wallet that holds 800 credit cards and weighs 38 pounds, but he has most of his cards inside a safety deposit box.[8]

The Diner's Club pioneered a new kind of lending, one that offered merchants a chance to be involved in the credit card purchasing method. When the prime rate hit 20 percent in 1981, credit card rates became high. The prime rate eventually came back down. But the banks found that consumers didn't really mind paying such a high rate of 18 to 22 percent, and they left the interest rate there, even until today. In fact, most department store credit card rates are between 19 and 26 percent.

These types of interest rates helped attract new players into the credit card arena, including Sears, Discover Card, MasterCard, Visa—and all kinds of competitors. With over 20,000 different kinds of credit cards on the market, they had to have a way to solicit new clients. It was no longer just the convenience of using a card. Now the credit cards moved into new competition, having different colors—gold, platinum, black—and other kinds of benefits like free travel insurance and lost cash advances, etc., etc.

So now credit card carrying and credit card usage helps people define their status in the social structure. But people who look at credit cards that way are forgetting a truth we've just learned on the preceding pages. They're forgetting what the banker knows. Because what the banker knows is that he doesn't care what color your credit card is. All he cares about is that you use the card and carry a big balance.

That's why, when I counsel clients about getting out of debt, I tell them to go "cold turkey"—that is, to stop charging immediately. "Tapering off" rarely works for smokers or spenders who need to quit. In our version of "plastic surgery," we literally cut the credit cards up and tell our clients that, until their finances are in order and secure, they're only to use a Visa debit card. Once they're on their feet financially, we tell them they can use one credit card, but they must be careful not to lean on it and overspend with it.

Additionally, they must always pay off their debt each month and keep track of their expenses to make sure they're not charging more than they can afford. Remember, credit cards are convenience tools not only for individuals, but also for banks because the banks know exactly what credit cards can do for them. And they know how to market them without mentioning all the possible fees you may incur. (Such fees brought in $34 billion in additional revenue in 2006.)[9]

Just remember, credit cards are the money changers' favorite money extraction tool. So avoid them at all cost unless you're in a position to pay them off each month. But credit cards are not the only strategy that the money changers use to make money.

A **finance company** is another lender that tends to take advantage of people who have a hard time borrowing from a bank. (Not being able to get a loan from your bank should tell you something about how much business you have trying to go deeper into debt.)

When we were first married, Drenda and I leaned heavily on debt when we didn't have the money to pay the bills. We first approached a finance company for help, but it wasn't long before we found ourselves unable to make the payment to them. When we asked for assistance, they were more than happy to delay the deadline for our payment and simply just began a new loan. We soon came to realize that in these types of loans, the interest is paid up front and that if you don't make your payments on time, they will recommend changing the payment terms while the interest starts back over. With interest rates typically between 24 and 32 percent, it's easy to see why it's next to impossible to ever repay the amount originally borrowed. For this reason, most finance companies could easily be considered modern-day loan sharks.

Again, lenders prey on people with a payment mentality and do not readily disclose in an understandable manner the true impact that interest and time have on repayment. My rule of thumb: stay away from finance companies.

Believe it or not, finance companies aren't the worst ones out there. Even more damaging to your financial health is the come-on from the lenders who offer **"payday loans."** These are loans that front you the money that should be yours come the next pay period. The interest rate, however, can be as high as 500+ percent!

Think about it. If a person is having a hard time making it from payday to payday on 100 percent of their pay, who would expect them to make it with a big bite taken out in interest? These insanely high interest rates put people on a speedy downward spiral. About this form of borrowing, the Center for Responsible Lending says:

> America's working families pay billions of dollars in excessive fees every year, as payday lenders across the nation routinely flip small cash advances into long-term, high-cost loans with annual interest rates in the range of 400%.[10]

An article that appeared in the *Denver Post* on Sept. 25, 2005, stated that on average payday loan customers end up paying 520% in finance fees on a typical loan.[11] The Center for Responsible Lending also says:

> Despite attempts to reform payday lending, now an industry exceeding $28 billion a year, lenders still collect 90% of their revenue from borrowers who cannot pay off their loans when due, rather than one-time users dealing with short-term financial emergencies.[12]

Incredibly, in a May 6, 2008 edition of *60 Minutes*, CBS stated that these lenders did not exist ten years ago in the United States but are now more numerous than McDonald's, setting up shop in every small town in America.

Sadly, what is meant to be a quick fix for a financial shortfall usually becomes a crushing, long-term problem. The money changers will always extend you more credit than you have any business receiving, but always at rates that make you poorer and them richer.

Another credit option that preys upon the struggling and the gullible is the **"car title loan."** Like payday loans, car title loans are marketed as small emergency loans, but in reality, these loans trap borrowers in a cycle of debt. A typical car title loan has a triple-digit annual interest rate, requires payment within one month, and is made for much less than the value of the car.

"Car title loans put at high risk an asset that is essential to the well-being of working families—their vehicle," explains the Center for Responsible Lending. "As the title to the car is on the line for typically small loans of several hundred dollars, it is a risk that should be avoided at all costs."[13] Jean Ann Fox, Director of Consumer Protection for the Consumer Federation of America cautions strongly against taking out a loan against your wheels:

> Car title pawns are really legalized car theft, because you lose the entire car equity no matter what the loan amount is. To put all of that at risk to borrow a few hundred dollars is just not fair.[14]

When not borrowing based on the equity in their vehicles, desperate people will turn to a much bigger source of equity—the roof over their heads. If other lines of credit have been maxed out or are in collection, homeowners often have no other source of available funds. People in this situation are frequently subject to **sub-prime loans** that exploit their situation with high interest rates and high fees.[15] Homeowners are constantly bombarded with advertising from lenders that want to "help them out" when times are tough. As an example of some of the claims made by banks in this area, I received a card from my bank promoting their second mortgages over other banks. It actually read: "Our second mortgage is better than most because we only charge interest, leaving you more money for the more important things in life." Right. As if paying my bills is not important. If all I were to do is pay only interest, my bank is ensuring that I'm paying on this debt for a *very* long time.

Lastly, **pawn shops** offer yet another way for you to trade your dollars for pennies. Pawn shops are often referred to as "loans of last resort." They are really just money lenders except that instead of accepting your car or home's equity, they settle for smaller goods such as jewelry, high-end watches, and electronics. You give them the goods, they give you money based upon a low-ball valuation of your goods. Of course, if you fail to make repayment for the loan within the established time period (and most people do), your valuables go on the open market at the pawn shop. Because so little value is placed upon the pawned items, the pawn broker can sell the goods at a greatly reduced price and still come out way ahead. For the broker, your borrowing from him is a winning situation. For you, not so much.

In the best case, you've borrowed against something of worth at a very high interest rate and later reclaimed your item; in the worst case, you've jeopardized something that would cost much more than you were lent.

As I mentioned, in our early years together, Drenda and I often found ourselves in need of cash in a fast manner. At times, we had no income and we would go to the pawn shop and leave our jewelry, guns, and other valuables in exchange for some quick cash. Unfortunately, the interest rates at most pawn shops are in the 200 to 300 percent range, making it extremely difficult to repay the original loan. As a result, we lost a lot of valuable things we had pawned because we couldn't afford to repay the loans.

The vital lesson of all these borrowing schemes is that if you're able to support all your purchases with real, honest-to-goodness money, you can avoid a lot of misery and poverty.

Lastly, the marketing ads that the money changers use to snare their victims should be considered an art. These strategies are deceptive and appeal only to emotion and not to common sense. Take for instance the "Coke a day" pitch. This strategy is frequently presented in sales pitches (usually those pushing subscriptions or memberships). In their appeal they promise their product or membership in their gym, vacation club, or insurance plan can be had, "for as little as the cost of a Coke a day." It's tempting to think that for the coins it takes to purchase a daily soft drink you could have “abs of steel,” “family vacations *forever!”* or “peace of mind knowing your family won’t be burdened.”

Tempting. But also very misleading.

In many ways this is even worse than credit card debt, because you’ll keep paying and paying as long as you want their product, service, or membership (which most people never take advantage of by the way). Again, the consumer just shrugs off the $10 a month fee as insignificant, but now you know the rest of that story.

A tactic similar to the “Coke a day” ploy is the “90 days same as cash” offer that has become so popular for big-ticket items like furniture, electronics, and mattresses. I’ve seen the down side of these agreements firsthand. I had a friend who, while his finances were a bit tight, was also in need of a computer. Thinking he was “just looking” for computers, he was quickly lured into buying one on the “12 months same as cash” plan. His reasoning was that he needed the computer now and that surely his financial situation would change for the better in the next year. But his financial picture didn’t change and the fine print contained in his financing agreement took effect. That’s when the interest rate he was paying jumped to 28 percent. Looking back, my friend admitted that he never should have gone into the store and bought the computer because he never would have bought anything expecting to pay 28 percent interest. Again, this is one of those fine details that shrewd lenders know and use to their advantage at our expense.

Remember, what appears as too good to be true for the consumer usually is. And usually such schemes bring very high interest payments with them. The general understanding with “same as cash” offerings is that you get the product today and can pay it out interest free within the preset time period. Of course, people rarely do. Then when you fail to pay the balance in full, you end up being charged a big, fat interest rate, one you would have never agreed to under *normal* circumstances.

Even worse, that rate is calculated from the original date of purchase, not the end of the designated time period. Even if you've made some partial payments toward your purchase, you're in for some very high payments to pay off that balance. If you're so completely sure you're going to have the money to make good on the debt in 90 days, wait the 90 days. Then make the purchase in full with cash.

Of all the money changer methods to take cash from the American family, I still believe the credit card is the most dangerous. Credit cards are still mostly unregulated and they continue to use attractive yet predatory lending techniques. It's easy to see why the typical American family is losing thousands and thousands of dollars to them every month. The modern-day money changers are definitely changing money, but it's not in your favor.

If you find yourself in deep credit card debt, I recommend an abrupt, and probably painful, cold-turkey cutoff. Do plastic surgery—cut the cards to bits and pieces and don't accept another offer until your finances are 100 percent in order and under control. Only then can you hope to use credit cards responsibly—as a convenience tool that eliminates the need to carry around substantial amounts of cash for everyday purchases.

If you just can't rise to the challenge of paying them off in full each month, as well as keeping an on-going record of your outstanding charges, you're not ready to have them again. For many, the safest and most direct path to staying out of debt is to operate on a cash-only basis.

There's no shame in operating like this. When you do, you are among the financial elite of our country and honoring God at the same time. That's a win-win situation for you.

chapter 4

troubled **times ahead**

As I was driving into town the other day, there was a road construction sign sitting near the pavement. There was also a flagger responsible for slowing the traffic and making sure people could navigate through the narrow, one-lane road they were allowed to traverse while the construction was taking place.

Everyone slowed down. Of course, the signs were put there so people could anticipate the construction before they got there. Without the signs they'd run the risk of hurting themselves or someone else. They would also incur a double fine for speeding through a construction zone.

However, in the area of finances there are signs all over the place warning people of an upcoming possible disaster. There's troubling news and troubling economic data on every front. But instead of slowing down, families and individuals are speeding up. They're borrowing more and more money, as though things will continue as they always have. Their debt continues, as well as their bondage.

One of those key indicators that warns of danger ahead and that things are changing permanently is the huge loss of manufacturing and service jobs in the United States. On a recent business trip I was seated next to a former BankOne executive, and he began telling me about the significant number of jobs in the banking industry that were being lost to overseas outsourcing. The most interesting part of this was that the jobs that were leaving our country were not entry-level roles, but high-paying, upper management positions.

As of 2007, one out of ten service jobs in the United States has been replaced by workers in China or India. Four to five million manufacturing/service jobs have been lost over the last six years to China, India, Asia, and the Third world via NAFTA, CAFTA, GATT, and WTO.[1] A University of California at Berkeley study suggests that 14 million jobs could be lost by 2015.[2] Citigroup is already ahead of most employers in this trend with 8,000 employees in India and abroad. Other companies with a significant number of foreign-based employees include Microsoft, IBM, Reebok, Sony, and Eastman Kodak. There are some pretty powerful pricing incentives behind this trend. For example, an architectural job that was bid by an American firm at $140,000 was bid by a competing firm in India at $12,000. That's a 91 percent savings.[3]

Altogether, these differences in production costs translated into a $856 billion dollar trade deficit in 2007. The trade deficit for October 2009, the first month of the U.S. fiscal year of 2010, was $176 billion. This is an annual rate of $2.1 trillion and represents one of the largest transfers of wealth in the history of the world.[4]

The indications of an economy on the brink of disaster are becoming harder and harder to ignore. There's dangerous territory ahead. And those who want to make it through these tough times will need to plan wisely for a shift in the economic winds. I share these statistics to help you understand the impending financial chaos that's coming to this country and to help solidify your desire to be out of debt.

In 1980 when I started my business, I only thought lots of Americans were in debt, not the majority. I didn't understand how big the debt problem was or how fast it was growing. At that time the total U.S.

national debt was $800 billion. Today, only 30 years later, it has grown to more than $13 trillion.[5] It is interesting that when I released the first edition of *Fixing the Money Thing* I reported a national debt of $9.4 trillion. An increase of $3.6 trillion has taken place in one and one-half years! Scott Minerd, who is the chief investment officer for Midland National Life and works with Guggenheim, a global, financial service firm stated in a recent financial conference that over the next five years the United States will add another $5 to 6 trillion to the national debt, which he warned is not sustainable. Even now tax receipts only cover the entitlement expenses in the nation; the rest must be borrowed. Current interest rates are near 0 percent, but if they rise, as they will surely do, the impact on the United States will be dramatic.[6]

In Harry Figgie's book *Bankruptcy 1995: The Coming Collapse of America and How to Stop It,* he indicates that the total debt in 1980, including all government, corporate, and personal debt, was $5.6 trillion.[7] At the end of 2006, that debt was $44 trillion or $88 trillion if unfunded liabilities were figured in.[8] The staggering fact is that this tremendous onslaught of debt has happened in just the last 26 years. Harry Figgie's predictions were simply delayed by low interest rates financing the nation's debt. The facts speak for themselves however: America is bankrupt!

Looking at a list of the top 163 nations of the world in regard to how *little* debt they carry, we find the United States at number 163, the largest debtor nation on the face of the earth and in history. At the top of the list is China, the first nation in history to ever accumulate over $1 trillion in cash.[9] It's no wonder the American dollar is sliding against other national currencies.

The McAlvany Intelligence Advisor quotes analyst Rob Arnott:

> The world has not seen such debt levels in modern history. This debt is not serviceable. Imagine, total debt is 557 percent of GDP, without considering entitlements. The interest on the debt will consume all the tax revenues of the country in the

not-too-distant future. Then there will be no way out but to create more debt in order to finance the old debt.[10]

"It is no secret that the nation is swimming—drowning—in borrowed cash," says Ken Bensinger of *SmartMoney.com.*[11] *CNN Money*, dated February 26, 2008, says that consumers rang up $2.2 trillion in new credit card debt in 2007 alone.[12] The nation seems bent on borrowing itself into a financial meltdown. The economic turmoil that has plagued the U.S. economy in just the last ten years has been unprecedented. Starting in 2000, America has been going through one of the greatest economic upheavals of her life, a financial crisis that has not been seen since the Great Depression of the early 1930s. From March of 2000 until March of 2003, $10 trillion vanished from the stock market. Certainly, the events of 9/11 played a key role in that decline, but the markets were already sliding six months before that date. More than 52 million households saw their retirement accounts decline by 50 to 70 percent. I've talked to some people who saw their retirement accounts drop 90 percent in the aftermath of the attacks on our country, and some were completely wiped out.

On top of that, we saw the fastest decline in fixed-rate interest rates in history as the government tried to lower interest rates and lower taxes to inject the economy with cash. This action alone caused millions of retirees, who depended on fixed-rate investments for income, to suddenly fall short of cash. Again, a few years later, the same kind of financial tsunami hit but with greater force as $14 trillion vanished from the markets in 2008 and 2009. It is incredible that in a nine-year period of time we have heard, "It hasn't been this bad since the Great Depression" twice!

During the first go-around, state revenues tanked with 38 states out of 50 becoming insolvent. California, being the largest, had a $38 billion deficit. California went so far as to actually kick the governor out in midterm to find someone who could take charge of the financial chaos. That same kind of chaos is again happening in 2010 as California, Arizona, Florida, Illinois, Michigan, Nevada, New Jersey, Oregon, Rhode

Island, and Wisconsin top the list of states with budget deficits. All 50 states combined report a $162 billion shortfall.[13] California is again the top loser with a deficit of 49.3 percent of revenues. The only reason we have not seen huge defaults is because the federal government came to the aid of the states and municipalities with free stimulus money. Those measures were temporary however and did not fix the underlying unemployment problem, and the states are again in Washington, DC, asking for more aid.

Speaking of aid, who would have ever thought they would see the day that the two largest banks in the United States, Citibank and Bank of America, would be on their knees begging for financial bailout money as occurred in 2008 and 2009? America's entire banking system is in a state of panic. A total of 237 banks in the United States have failed since 2008, 72 in the first five months of 2010. *The Wall Street Journal* reported on May 21, 2010 that 775 more banks are in danger of closing up shop.[14] That number represents 10 percent of all the banks in the nation. Maybe you should read that last sentence again just to make sure you read it right—I know that I had to.

Besides seeing problems with government deficits and bank failures, we have seen tremendous corporate upheavals, as two-thirds of the companies on the S&P 500 became insolvent in regard to their own pension funds, which the government, by the way, was obligated to back up with tax dollars.

General Motors, the largest of these cases, owed its own pension fund $13 billion, almost one-half of its entire value in 2004. Of course, GM's problems did not end in 2004. They kept going and going, losing $10.5 billion in 2005. In 2006 they laid off 30,000 people, closed 12 plants, and lost $3 billion through the first nine months of the year.[15]

Eventually, General Motors had to borrow $60 billion to stay in business during 2009. Based on their current sales forecast, the taxpayers were asked to subsidize every car they sold with about $12,200 per car to keep the company's doors open.[16] How about Chrysler? They had thirteen thousand layoffs and two North American plant closures. Operations lost $1.5 billion in 2006, with prospects so dire that the company began to look for assets to sell in 2007. On the verge of going under, they too received government money to the tune of $17.4 billion. It should also be noted that the federal government also kicked in $2 billion for the "cash for clunkers" program as well as many loans to help the automakers retool.

The government's solution to these problems that surfaced in 2001 and 2007 was the same: drive interest rates down and pump trillions of dollars into the economy. The result of that strategy in 2001 and 2002 was a huge real estate price bubble fueled by the easy money, which caused the total residential debt in the United States to climb from $4 trillion to $12 trillion *in just five years*. Credit rules were relaxed and people could qualify for a mortgage with no verified documents. If a person had a job, he or she could get a mortgage. Teaser rates or entry rates were low, and 25 percent of the residential mortgage market used these variable interest rate loans to get into houses they could not afford. As rates went up and these loans reset, thousands of mortgages began to default.

This bubble implosion again set off an even bigger global crisis. So again, the federal government lowered interest rates to 0 percent to avert a meltdown and pumped trillions of dollars into the economy, this time into Wall Street, the big banks, and the financial system. The result was a stock market rise of 50 percent in 2009. But this stock market rise is all based on the huge cash infusions that came from the $787 billion economic stimulus package, the $702 billion TARP program, the $43 billion the government used to prop up Bank of America, the $50.8 billion they used to prop up Citigroup, and the $200 billion used in the government takeover of Freddie Mac and Fannie Mae. But again, we have to ask if this rise is based on solid economic recovery or speculation. I think the graph below will help you see what I am talking about.

The following graph shows the homes that were on the market at the end of March of 2010. You can see that in 2008 the number of homes on the market skyrocketed. You then see that spike started to fall rapidly. In case you are wondering why, that is when the government began to do two things. First, they paid banks for their bad loans and the banks began to short sell them at huge loses. (My daughter recently bought a home for $50,000 that appraised in 2006 for $195,000.) Second, the government offered home buyers $8,500 to help purchase their homes.

At the end of 2009, however, that line shot back up. What happened there? Well, the $8,500 home buyer's credit ran out and housing sales stopped. So the government extended it and the spike turned back down. The fact is that most of these government cash infusion programs are coming to an end soon, so we will see what happens to the markets. As this chapter is being written the markets are down for 2010 with May being the worst May on record since 1940.

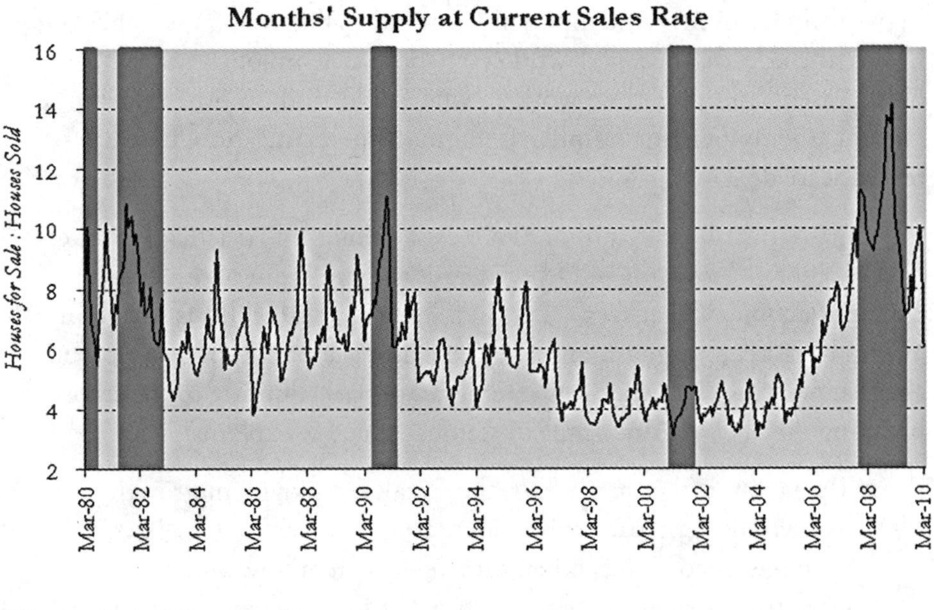

Source: US Census Bureau, Bloomberg, NBER

9

We can get an idea of how unstable the whole system is by a dramatic event that occurred on May 6, 2010. The stock market crashed in a one-day free fall that set a record, over 1,000 points down. The day it happened, the feds tried to downplay the event as if there was some kind of computer error. Only Fox News reported it correctly that the turmoil in Greece and the shaky economy caused the crash. The whole thing became unraveled when a hedge fund, Universa Investments L.P., bought 50,000 options contracts that would net them $4 billion if the S&P fell to 800 during the month of June.[17] The S&P was currently trading at 1145 on May 6th. In case you have not calculated it yet, that is a 30 percent drop in value. When other trading floors saw the bet, they responded themselves and bingo—panic. If Universa thought that it was possible for a 30-day drop of 30 percent and bet on that, I think we also need to think that it is possible as well.

Let's put a little more perspective into our story. Since 2007 Americans have lost 1.7 million homes, 8 million jobs and over $14 trillion in wealth. Currently unemployment stands at about 9 percent, but if you include discouraged workers (whose unemployment payments have ceased) and part-time workers who could find no other work, the current unemployment number is about 18 percent.[19] So where are we really headed?

Christian E. Weller, author of a recent Center for American Progress (CAP) report "Drowning in Debt," details the end result of this continued course of action. Weller says, "The middle class, specifically, is struggling. Wages have been stagnant and they're losing the battle to keep up with the cost of living."[19] Weller sees several factors contributing to the record-breaking number of Americans in serious debt. He explains:

> The labor market has been rather weak, employment growth has barely kept pace with population growth, wages have been flat, income has fallen for five years in a row, and at the same time, prices for critical big ticket items—items such as health care, housing, college education—have gone through

> the roof. In that bind, the only escape valve for middle class families is to borrow more money.
>
> The scope of the problem is large and it's growing. We now have the highest level of debt relative to income on record since the 1950's. We also have the highest debt payments (including interest and principle) relative to income since the 1980's. We're in a unique world that we've never seen before, and what's surprising is that we've reached these levels in a time of historically low interest rates. So from that perspective, you know that going forward, our debt levels can only go up.[20]

Not exactly a promising future for the "land of plenty," is it?

New York bankruptcy attorney Warren R. Graham goes a step further in his dire predictions for the American economy when he says:

> A weakening housing market, together with other financial currents in the U.S. economy, represents the potential final impetus to a "perfect storm" brewing over the American middle class....[21]

In a commentary more than a decade ago, *USA Today* writer Steve Slavin wrote:

> America is being transformed from an industrial colossus to a tired, down-at-the-heels, post-industrial society. For years, many poor nations have come with tin cups and begged for loans and outright grants. The U.S. has gone from being the world's biggest creditor nation to the number-one debtor....
>
> What the U.S. has been doing these last 15 years is mortgaging the future for the present. Americans are indulging themselves in consumer goods—many supplied by foreigners—and incurring a huge national debt because they refuse to tax themselves for a growing proportion of what

> the Federal government spends. Americans are running up a huge tab and leaving it for future generations.[22]

It's frightening to realize this was written 17 years ago when our country's financial footing was much sounder than it is today. As if to echo Slavin's on-the-mark financial predictions, writer Mike Whitney asserts in an article entitled "Day of Reckoning: America's Economic Meltdown": "There's a growing concern among economists and market-savvy pundits that the global financial system is hanging by a few well-worn threads that could snap at any time..."[23]

Even those on the "inside" such as Government Accountability Office chief David M. Walker are talking doom and gloom. "This is about the future of our country, our kids, and grandkids," he says. Walker has taken to traveling the country to tell of what he sees as a "demographic tsunami" that will come when the Baby Boom generation begins retiring and the recklessness of borrowing money from foreign lenders comes due.[24]

Walker and his team of experts that travel with him have a simple, yet sobering message:

> If the United States government conducts business as usual over the next few decades, a national debt that is already $13 trillion could reach $46 trillion or more, adjusted for inflation. That's almost as much as the total net worth of every person in America—Bill Gates, Warren Buffet, and those Google guys included. A hole that big could paralyze the U.S. economy. According to some projections, just the interest payments on a debt that big would be as much as all the taxes the government collects today. And, every year that nothing is done about it, the problem grows by $2 trillion to $3 trillion.[25]

Just like her live-for-today-minded citizens, America as a country has spent like a drunken sailor in recent years, to the point of running up an annual $856 billion trade deficit by 2007. The possibility exists that number could be over 1 trillion in 2010. This means that the United States *imported* that much more in goods and services than it *exported*. "When the U.S. buys more than it sells, it makes up the difference, known as the trade deficit, by shipping dollars overseas. And in recent years it has been buying a lot more than it's been selling," says James Turk, a contributor to *The Daily Reckoning*.[26] He explains further:

> Why is America buying so much more than it's selling? One reason is that it's a lot cheaper to make most basic products in places like China, where smart, highly-motivated people will work for about a tenth of the prevailing U.S. wage. So U.S. companies, in order to take advantage of this differential, are closing factories here and setting up new ones over there.
>
> Powerhouse discount-store chains, Wal-Mart especially, are driving the process by buying from a growing network of Chinese plants, and passing some of the savings along to the customers, and either driving competitors out of business or forcing them to buy from cheap foreign sources as well. As a result, low-wage foreign factories are now flooding the United States with incredibly cheap stuff, much of which used to be made in the States.[27]

As the largest single importer of foreign-produced goods in the United States, Wal-Mart has served to undercut domestic manufacturing on a tremendous level. You don't have to be too old to remember those patriotic labels boasting "Made in the U.S.A." that so many Wal-Mart products used to proudly proclaim. Apparently, a few dollars saved on a Crock-Pot have cost us deeply in leverage in the world's economy. It's sad to realize that the appeal of lower costs of goods sold won out over patriotism with our fellow Americans.

As representative to the thousands of people impacted by these shifts in production allegiance, the AFL-CIO claims that more than

1.78 million manufacturing jobs have been replaced by foreign factory workers since 1998.[28] For white-collar workers, the investment firm Goldman Sachs estimates "400,000-600,000 professional services and information sector jobs have moved overseas in the last few years."[29] It seems no level of worker is exempt from the threat of losing their job to "offshoring," the newly created word that's industry-speak for foregoing American jobs for the sake of cheaper flip-flops. Or microwaves. Or computers. What is not fully explained behind the word *offshoring* is the implication it brings with it in the form of workers finding themselves priced out of a job by competitors half a world away or entire communities destitute due to plant closings. Warnings, warnings everywhere and yet the cheaper-priced housewares, lawn and garden supplies, and automotive products triumph every time.

In addition to the skyrocketing overall trade deficit, our country's huge appetite for oil continues.

As I write, the price of oil has topped $86 per barrel in 2010. But two years ago it hit a record $140 per barrel before the current economic crisis. Although oil has indeed retreated in price, we need to keep the price in perspective. Just eight years ago, oil was only $26 a barrel. Amazingly, in September of 2007 oil was at $70 a barrel, yet by May of 2008 it reached a price of over $120 a barrel. Then a few months later it hit $140 per barrel. A *USA Today* article dated June 27th, 2008 made headlines when it said that oil could reach $170 a barrel before the end of 2008.[30] Of course that did not happen, but that speculation was based on factual assumptions. America is now dependent on foreign oil with 75 percent of the oil that America uses coming from foreign sources. About 23.5 percent of that oil is imported from the Persian Gulf.

The point I want to make is, although America only has 300 million people, she uses 25 percent of the world's production of oil and is the largest user of oil in the world as a percentage of total production. In comparison, I'd like you to think a minute about the size of China and India with a combined population of 2.4 billion—not million but billion—people. Economic production capacity is growing in those countries at a rate of more than 8 to 11 percent a year, and almost all that production is using oil-based energy. In China the sale of passenger cars and other light vehicles grew nearly 50 percent in 2009 causing China to pass the United States as the largest automotive market. That market is set to continue to explode as only 35 out of 1,000 people own a car in China compared to 439 per 1,000 people in the U.S.[31]

What would happen if these countries wanted to enjoy the standard of living to which U.S. citizens have become accustomed? The current production capacity of the raw materials for that to happen is not currently in place, so production would be unable to keep up with demand. The result would be what we have seen in 2007 and what we will be seeing in the future: rising commodity prices across the world.

Over the last few years China has become the largest consumer of copper, iron ore, zinc, tin, rubber, wool, cotton, coal, aluminum, and platinum, and is the second largest consumer of oil behind the United States. The amazing fact is that China was an oil exporter only eight years ago, and now she's become a large importer.[32]

In the same way as the rising global demand for oil is driving prices up, so the fast growth in other economies of the world will cause the prices of other commodities to jump as well. Because of this, in December of 2006 the U.S. Mint implemented regulations making it illegal to melt American nickels and pennies, which cost about 2 cents for a penny and 9 cents for a nickel to produce.[33] If someone were to manufacture these, melt these down, or try to send them across our borders, they could receive a fine of $10,000, five years in jail, or both. With these facts in mind, you need to be prepared to understand that commodities, the things you take for granted, are only going to go up in price over the next few years.

There's another thing you need to be aware of that I think could have disastrous consequences for the United States. As I have already mentioned, the current U.S. national debt stands at more than $13 trillion.

What you may not know is that currently foreigners own most of this debt. That means the bills, the bonds, and the notes that America sells to fund its debt are being held by foreign governments and investors.

As America's economy slumps and other nations' economies surge, America's dollar is being devalued across the world. As the dollar is devalued, the U.S. dollars that other countries hold lose value. In fact, the dollar has fallen 30 percent against other currencies in the last five years.[34] This decline in value could be higher than the interest rate being paid on those bonds. So in reality, those who are holding U.S. bonds are receiving a negative return. The nations that are holding those bonds are seeking to reduce their exposure to the falling U.S. dollar and invest in currencies that are rising, or they are fleeing now to gold. As these countries begin to reduce their holdings of U.S. bonds, the demand for these bonds will decline at the U.S. Treasury auctions, thus causing interest rates to rise in the United States and promoting possible recessional pressures in the U.S. economy.

The warning signs are growing by the day: personal bankruptcies increasing, corporate pensions losing their value, jobs being eliminated, rising oil prices, service and manufacturing jobs leaving the country, devaluing of the U.S. dollar abroad, and the increasing debt load speak loudly that things are changing.

And it all adds up to one thing: The time to get out of debt is now. The time to rein in out-of-control spending is now. The time to quit spending all you get and start saving for the future is now. It's not next week, next month, or when your over-the-top consumption has finally led you to exhaust all reasonable financial options.

Friends, that elusive some day is ***today!***

For the sake of your personal health and well-being, for the sake of our country's future in what has become a global economy, and most importantly, for the sake of honoring your relationship with our Lord, *stop!* Stop today and break what is surely a vicious cycle of spending, worrying, spending more, worrying more, and so on. The Lord would much rather have you expend your energies working for His Kingdom rather than working endless hours for endless weeks only to have enough money to buy a new DVD player—a DVD player that almost certainly bears the label "Made in China."

chapter 5

what no one wants you to know

As the previous chapters revealed, there are perilous times ahead. Everyone should take any necessary adjustments to avoid becoming a financial victim in the years ahead.

Again, the best way to avoid that unpleasant picture in your future is to get out of debt.

That thought may still bring skepticism on your part. But what if I told you that you could be debt free, including your home mortgage, in five to seven years without changing your income? Would you be overjoyed and ask me to reveal "the secret"? Or would you write me off as someone "telling tales" that are too good to be true?

For the sake of your financial well being, I hope you stay with me through this chapter and hear me through until the end. Remember that no matter what I claim can be a reality for you, it can also be backed up by basic arithmetic. In other words, what I'm going to show you is a financial reality, and you can prove it to yourself with a simple calculator.

Before I share the inside secret that so many companies and lenders wish to keep from you, you have to first understand their motivations.

You see, if you really grab hold of this concept, you may never need to borrow again. That can be terrific news to you and your family. But the folks at MasterCard, Discover, and Visa would be out of work if everyone were to embrace this simple practice. Not only that, all the home mortgage lenders and finance companies would also find themselves with a lot less business too. The people in advertising would also find their services in much less demand if all we did was stop buying things we couldn't pay cash for.

So back to my original proposition: Would you think it possible to rid yourself of debt, including your home mortgage, without increasing your income, in as little as five to seven years? For the typical American—buried under a mountain of credit card debt and dragging around a jumbo, low-equity home mortgage—the possibility of complete and total financial freedom is just a daydream. And in most minds, it's about as likely as winning the Mega-Power-Super lottery.

The fact is, the odds of hitting the lottery jackpot are even longer than you can imagine. But your chances for success with my financial freedom plan are actually very, very good. Even better, *you can control* whether or not you "win" in my financial exercise. You can't control the lottery. Pay close attention to the following example to see how you truly can take control of your financial future. No matter how radical you find my plan, you have to admit, it's considerably more responsible and more rational than foolishly staking your welfare on a random lottery drawing.

I always tell my clients that it is possible to pay cash for their homes and I'm always, *always* met with disbelief that such a significant purchase can be made without the use of borrowed funds. I encourage them and then proceed to "do the math." Watch closely.

If you were to purchase a starter home for $121,000, you can either write the seller a check (what a great way to pay!) or visit your local lending institution and begin completing mountains of paperwork and commit to paying for this beginning home for the next 30 years. Hmmmmmm…which appeals to you more?

If all you had done was put $1,000 in savings once a month for seven years and drawn an average rate of return of 10 percent, (Note: 2010 average market rates of return would be hard pressed to earn 10% but 10% is being used as an example to make the point clear) you'd be able to write that check and own the home free and clear of any debt. With your cumulative total investment of $84,000 ($1,000/month x 12 months/year x 7 years = $84,000) plus the interest of $37,627 (10 percent compounded daily for 7 years) you would have some powerful negotiating power: a total of $121,627 in real, honest-to-goodness cash.

That's seven years of sacrifice versus thirty years of debt!

I will be the first to admit that putting away $1,000 a month is much easier said than done, but when you consider the alternative of traditional financing, the difference is staggering. Assume you enter into an agreement to purchase the same home, but with no money to put toward the purchase price. Additionally, assume you are now paying that same 10 percent interest rate to finance your loan. (Note: Compared with current lending rates at the time of this writing, 10 percent is a high interest rate to pay for financing a home loan, but this rate was selected for consistency in the comparison.)

If financed over the traditional 30-year period, this starter home would end up costing you $382,273 over the life of the loan! That's over three times the amount you wanted to pay for the house. If you were in a 28 percent tax bracket while you were earning that $382,273, the taxes would add an additional $148,661 to the total price of the house. This brings the total price of the house to $530,934. No wonder most people never pay off their houses. With a net take-home wage of $50,000 a year, it would take 11 years to pay off the house if every single penny you earned went to pay for the mortgage during that 11-year period. Your choice here is to pay $84,000 (that is the total principal that you invested during the seven year $1,000 investment) or pay $530,934.

Let me give one final example to drive home the savings power that "cash in hand" truly can be. Say you're set to purchase this same $121,000 starter home, but instead of saving for the seven years *prior* to the purchase, you intend to borrow the money. Let's also assume that you want to spend that same $1,000 a month that you could have saved for the seven years prior to purchasing the house, but you didn't. Since it will take $1,061 a month to pay off the house in the 30-year mortgage and that payment is $61 per month higher than what you have, guess what? The house will never be paid off, *never!* So now you choose, save $1,000 a month for seven years or spend $1,000 a month forever.

For me, for you, for the millions of hardworking mothers and fathers just trying to "get by," the first step toward getting out of debt is to reeducate ourselves about *all* the financial possibilities that exist. The fact is that we have all been brainwashed to believe that the debt system is the system of choice. No one really believes that they can be free. Instead, everyone focuses on payment amounts, not cash. For Drenda and me, this reeducation began as soon as we came to the agreement that we were finished with living in debt. We decided that we were going to trust God to teach us His system. Not surprisingly, the Lord was standing by ready and willing. The Holy Spirit soon began His work.

Soon my mind began to have thoughts I'd never thought before. In the night, when I was lying in my bed, the Holy Spirit would bring ideas and concepts to me that I had never thought possible. I couldn't shake these ideas. Eventually I started playing with and meditating on these new concepts. I was shocked one day, playing with my financial calculator, to find out that a family that I was currently working with could be out of debt in less than seven years, including their home mortgage, on their current income. At first I thought I must have made a mistake. I went through my numbers again and again. I recalculated the same plan over and over again, and to my amazement, I found out that my calculations were correct.

The family I had been meeting with was in trouble financially. They were living month to month as most Americans in debt do. But amazingly, these financial concepts the Holy Spirit was showing me could help not just me or this particular family, but *anyone* else pay off his or her mortgage and credit cards in just a few years. How could I keep this exciting and freeing information just to myself? The answer was, I couldn't.

When I went back to the clients' home, I had prepared a neat printout of what I had discovered. I had found that by simply rearranging some financial priorities and by making a few changes that freed up monthly cash flow, they could be completely out of debt in five to seven years. This included their mortgage *and* didn't require an increase in income.

Their response was about the same as mine had been—complete shock. They simply couldn't believe it. To fully convince them, I had to go through the numbers several times and verify it was true. To this day, I can still see the look of shock and awe on my clients' faces as they came to realize that my calculations were correct. The joy and excitement they experienced was incredible. They realized that they were not destined to be slaves to debt but that they could actually be free.

Later that night when I returned to my office, I pulled the files of some of my other clients and began working through the information I had on their finances. Incredibly, almost every family whose finances I analyzed that night could also be out of debt in the five- to seven-year range, again, including their mortgages and without increasing their incomes. What an exciting night that was to discover this tremendous secret that *no one* seemed to know.

For the short-term, I maintained my commission-based job selling insurance products. However, as I visited with each client about my employer's products, I also shared my findings about living the debt-free life. It wasn't long before I had a business opportunity right before my eyes that I couldn't possibly walk away from.

I should tell you that months before this exciting time, the Lord had spoken to both Drenda and me on separate occasions. After praying late one night, Drenda was told that we would own a business aimed at helping couples with both their marriages and their finances. The Lord spoke this to her when we were still in desperate debt. I can still remember the night that she woke me up after praying for hours and excitedly told me what the Lord had said. I simply stared at her and said, "Well, if that's true I wish He'd tell me how to get out of debt first." Then I rolled over in bed with no further discussion of it and went to sleep. I was still in so much financial stress at the time that I just found what she said unbelievable.

Later the Lord gave me a dream showing me that I was indeed going to have a business helping people get out of debt. I had to apologize to Drenda for my inconsiderate response the night she woke me up because what Drenda had heard in prayer became a reality. So Drenda and I launched out on our own and started our business. I hired a computer programmer, and together he and I walked through the plan that I was currently putting together for my clients showing them how to be out of debt. He developed a data entry system and a finished plan I could use in my business presentations. I then began to hire others in my business to help me. Thus started the beginnings of the business I still own today, which now produces millions of dollars a year and helps thousands of people get out of debt.

Again and again, people were amazed at the simple truth that they could be free. I'd never done something that was so rewarding. As the new business prospered, we prospered and paid off all our debts in a couple of years. How amazing that something really so very simple, so readily available to all, was hidden from so many.

This privilege of helping others become debt free has lasted 22 years and is still going strong. Since beginning, tens of thousands of families have been ministered to and billions of dollars in interest have been saved by families who followed the same plan that I discovered. Although the plan is powerful yet simple, by itself it has no power to set people free. I learned that unless I taught people how to live without debt they would eventually continue to use it.

The solution was to teach the same answer that Drenda and I had discovered. And that was to trust God and His Kingdom for our provision. I found out, however, that many people, even Christians, did not know how to actually tap into the vast potential they have in the Kingdom of God. So any time we shared with people the simple plan to financial freedom we would always give them some instruction about the Kingdom.

Read on and we will do the same for you.

the revolution

chapter 6

common sense & **spiritual law**

Mention the word "inheritance" and many people immediately think of long-lost relatives leaving untold riches to them simply because they share a common last name. Bulging bank accounts, huge estates, and exotic cars come to mind too. But whether you realize it or not, you too have a family tie that entitles you to untold riches and an estate the likes of which you've never imagined. The exciting part of this story is that "the relative" doesn't have to be distant at all but, rather, can be a constant companion.

This relative, of course, is our Heavenly Father. And the inheritance part? Galatians 4:1 says, "*...as long as the heir is a child, he is no different from a slave, although he owns the whole estate.*" The chapter continues with verses 4-5 saying, "*...God sent His Son, born of a woman, born under law, to redeem those under law that we might receive the full rights of sons.*"

Just exactly what are "the full rights of sons?" Verses 6-7 tell us clearly:

> *Because you are sons, God sent the Spirit of His Son into our hearts, the Spirit who calls out, "'Abba,' Father." So you are no*

*longer a slave, but a son; and since you are a son, God has made you also an heir (*Galatians 4:6-7).

Let that soak in for a moment. God is giving you access to provision that is the birthright of those who have made Jesus the Lord of their lives and have become the sons and daughters of God. Think about that—this inheritance is never-ending, open to all, and eternal. That's something even the wealthiest of relatives can't leave you. Jesus summed it up very well when He said in Luke 6:20: *"...Blessed are you who are poor, for yours is the kingdom of God."* Very simply, Jesus was saying that the poor do not need to be poor anymore. They have now come into a new Kingdom with a new inheritance that wasn't limited by their daddy's last name.

I knew only too well the meaning of Lamentations 3:17 when it says, *"I have been deprived of peace; I have forgotten what prosperity is."* For a time there was no peace in my life. There's no peace when your babies need food that you can't buy, when you live in a constant whirlwind of financial stress struggling to survive on a daily basis. But as I began to discover the Kingdom of God and how to apply it to my life, my life was transformed.

As I began to live out these principles in my life, I wanted to tell everyone I came in contact with about the Kingdom. As I worked with families in my financial planning business, many who were on the brink of financial ruin, I suddenly realized that their financial futures were no longer exclusively dependent on their abilities to manage the financial ideas I brought them. Instead, I came to realize that many of them didn't know of the inheritance that was theirs as children of God. I knew that I had to tell them of this new Kingdom if I was ever going to permanently change their financial lives.

I was able to show them that by putting Kingdom principles into place, they too could access their inheritance and see the same dramatic changes that my family saw. Before long, people could see the changes that were taking place in my life financially. When I had the chance,

I would tell anyone who would listen about the Kingdom that I had discovered. Family and friends were my first audience. But before long I was being invited to speak to organizations and churches about the financial principles that had so changed my life. Everywhere I went, people were the same—stressed out over money, in debt, and desperately looking for answers. They wanted to know how they too could experience the freedom from debt that I was enjoying.

One of the most exciting stories we witnessed in those early days took place when I received a phone call from a man I'll call "Don," who was facing some severe financial issues. He had heard that I helped people with their finances.

When I first met Don, he had come to my office very discouraged and in debt. Nothing seemed to be going right in his life at the time. When I sat down and talked to him, I found out he was three to four months behind on his rent and on almost every other bill he had. There were marriage issues—his wife was fed up with their financial situation and had begun to lose respect for Don as he was unable to provide for her and their five children. The fact was, Don had lost respect for himself. And he was full of questions.

His then-current job involved selling health insurance across the state of Ohio, but his lack of success was quickly leading him down a disastrous financial path.

Despite all the things going against Don, I saw potential in him. He was willing to learn and willing to work. That powerful combination intrigued me enough to hire him and invest myself in the welfare of his future. In the end, it was an investment that paid huge dividends for both of us.

My fledgling company had just won a trip to Hawaii from one of our vendors and I felt this would be a great chance to share with Don about the Kingdom of God. Although Don was a Christian, he didn't have the same understanding I did. And although I'd tried on several occasions to share God's principles with him in this area, he just didn't seem to believe what I was saying.

I kept looking for a way to catch Don's attention that would help him realize that he too could have success by learning how God's Kingdom worked. However, Don was so discouraged that he had a hard time believing in himself and believing that change could really happen. I knew this Hawaii trip was my chance.

In the weeks before Don and I were to leave, we talked of what we would see and do there. One special interest held Don's attention like none other. He wanted to catch a blue marlin in the beautiful waters of the Pacific Ocean. "Hawaii is the blue marlin capital of the world," Don told me excitedly. "I've always wanted to catch a blue marlin; it's been a dream of mine." For the first time in weeks, I saw a gleam in Don's eyes. Something actually got him excited and I knew his excitement would open the door to a powerful lesson.

"Don," I said, "did you know that it is possible to know, not hope, but *know* that you will catch a blue marlin in Hawaii by tapping into the Kingdom of God?" Confused but intrigued, Don wanted to know more, and I continued with my explanation about the Kingdom. I quoted Mark 11:24 which says, *"Therefore I tell you, whatever you ask for in prayer, believe that you have received it, and it will be yours."* For Don this was almost too good to believe. I took some time to help him understand the Kingdom and how to release his faith. And so, before we left on our trip, he and his wife prayed in agreement and believed that they had received a blue marlin. They also sowed a financial seed into the Kingdom of God toward their harvest.

This was something the Holy Spirit had taught me to do when I released my faith for something that I needed. In the meantime Don did everything he knew to do to uphold his part of the harvest. He did some research on available boats and prices and finally booked with a captain that he felt good about. Everything was set and we were all so excited about going to the blue waters of Hawaii.

Sail day arrived, and as we boarded the boat we elatedly told the captain that today was the day we were going to catch a marlin. While he expected us to have a successful day fishing for other sport fish, he assured us the odds were not in our favor for catching a blue marlin that day. With two boats on chartered tours every day for the last four months, his crews had only brought in one blue marlin. This was due largely to the fact that it wasn't marlin season yet since marlin are a migratory fish. Refusing to be discouraged, we respectfully told him that we were going to receive one and continued getting our gear ready.

After six hours of trolling we hadn't had a single strike, and I was getting a bit worried that the lack of action might weaken Don's faith. In my concern I yelled out a question to him. "Don?" I yelled from my perch on the bridge above him, "Let me ask you a question. When did you receive that blue marlin? When it shows up or when we prayed?" In confidence, Don strongly replied, "Gary, that's simple. I received it when I prayed." I was excited and confident when I heard his reply. It was then that I knew Don had taken my instruction seriously and he was determined to have that marlin.

Minutes later, Don's reel began to sing as it bent seaward and the mates yelled, "Fish on!"

"Don't get too fired up," cautioned the captain, "It's a big fish all right, but it's no blue marlin. Marlins come right to the surface and make tremendous jumps through the air and this fish is staying deep." The minutes wore on as Don continued to wrestle with the fish that had yet to come close enough to the surface to be seen. As tired as Don was, the fish was more so and soon gave up the fight. Don and I weren't surprised as he reeled in that big, beautiful blue marlin, but everyone else on the boat was stunned.

The picture of Don and his fish remains in my office to this day as testimony to others and a constant reminder to me of the reality of the Kingdom. On the outside it was just a fish. But to Don the marlin meant so much more. If the Kingdom worked for the marlin, it would certainly work for everything else he needed in life. For Don it was just the beginning of realizing the impact the Kingdom of God could have on his life.

Go back a few thousand years and you'll learn about a man named Nicodemus, who questioned Jesus specifically about the Kingdom of God. Chapter 3 of the Book of John records the Lord's response, *"The wind blows wherever it pleases. You hear its sound, but you cannot tell where it comes from or where it is going. So it is with everyone born of the Spirit"* (John 3:8). That beautiful day aboard the boat with Don is as good an example of this as there will ever be.

While neither Don nor I could actually see the Kingdom of God, we certainly saw and felt its effect as that big marlin came in that day. Just like the wind cannot be seen but has a visible effect on the natural realm, so the Kingdom of God is real and has effect in the natural realm. By learning the laws that govern the Kingdom of God, we effect change in our lives just as Don did that day.

Another client I had the privilege of sharing the Kingdom of God with was a friend of mine, Johnny, and his wife. Their financial outlook was pretty grim and growing darker by the day. More than $5,000 behind on their bills, they had no prospect of any immediate income as their commission-based business was floundering. They called me and asked if I could stop by and talk to them about the Kingdom of God and finances. As we sat down, I began to explain exactly how the Kingdom works and how anyone can learn to walk in the Kingdom with victory. After a couple of hours I felt they were ready to release their faith and asked them, "What do you have?" They replied that all they had left was $160. "Instead of spending that money, let's release it as seed. Let's tap into our inheritance and let's believe God," I counseled them.

Just as I asked Johnny exactly how much he felt they needed, the Holy Spirit stopped me and said, "Do not let them answer. Instead ask if $12,000 would be enough." So I asked him if $12,000 would take care of his needs. I could see his eyes get big as the amount shocked him.

He had never made $12,000 in one month before in his business. After some discussion, he and his wife agreed that they would believe God for $12,000 in the next 30 days in their business.

Three weeks later he called to report that his business was booming. Clients were actively seeking him out rather than the other way around. Not only were they calling, but they were buying—to the tune of $17,000 that month! Again, we couldn't actually see and touch the Kingdom of God, but my friend saw and undoubtedly experienced the effects of the Kingdom in that unforgettable 30-day period. This was a powerful lesson for my friend—one he needed to remember and draw on in the days ahead.

From that powerful learning experience in January his business began to prosper. In May of that year, he was involved in a serious car accident that could have killed him. He had to be life-flighted to a nearby hospital. Because of the accident, he could not work for three months. When you make your living in a commission-based business, being laid up can be disastrous. In fact, he fell behind on his bills again.

During this time Johnny and his wife decided to move to Ohio and attend my church. They figured that since their business was down and they had to rebuild it anyway, they wanted to move and start over with us in Ohio. He found someone to rent out his home and rented a home here in Ohio. Unfortunately, once he was here the renter he had in Georgia left without notice and left him with a house payment there as well as the one he now had in Ohio.

Although his business was producing income again, he was still having a hard time catching up with the past-due bills and staying current on the home in Georgia. The lesson that he had learned earlier regarding the Kingdom was about to be tested again. This time Johnny knew how to release his faith in God's Word, and he did so knowing that he was going to pull out of this situation. His home in Georgia was now a few weeks away from foreclosure. Although it had been on the market for months, no one was buying and no one was renting.

The original adjustable rate mortgage payment of $800 had now ballooned to almost $2,000 a month as interest rates and taxes had gone up. Johnny just did not have the cash to bring it current. At the same time, the real estate market crashed as the sub-prime mortgage crisis hit America. His home was now barely worth what he owed on it, and people just were not buying. At the last minute, with two weeks to go before foreclosure, a man called and bought the house. Amazingly, the man offered Johnny $10,000 more than the list price if Johnny would take the house off the market for a month while he got his affairs in order to purchase it. He went ahead and sent Johnny the $10,000 to hold the house and this gave Johnny the money to bring the house current.

This by itself was extraordinary. Not only did someone buy the house at the last minute, but they also offered $10,000 more than he was asking and went ahead and wired that $10,000 on up to Johnny. At the same time, Johnny needed a new car. He had lost his car in the accident and the family was left driving an older van with 160,000 miles on it. The family was believing for a new vehicle.

Two weeks after the house was sold, Johnny received a call from an old schoolmate and neighbor. He was startled to hear his childhood friend ask an odd question: "Johnny, do you remember when you gave me your bicycle when we were twelve?"

"Yes," Johnny told him. "I remember that."

"Well, I want to repay you for that. I am going to buy you a BMW automobile."

Johnny couldn't believe what he was hearing. His friend was true to his word and in a few weeks sent Johnny a check. Instead of buying the BMW, Johnny decided that his family really needed two vehicles. So he went out and bought a Suburban and an Acura RL. Johnny said one night he went out to the driveway and just sat in the cars in thankfulness and shock. He had a hard time comprehending that both of those cars were his, really his. Both were fully paid for with cash.

Two weeks later, Johnny had spotted a farm home that he was interested in and he told me about it. I reminded Johnny that his credit was not good due to having fallen behind on his mortgage in Georgia. Furthermore, he had no down payment. I encouraged him to wait, build his business, and get some cash saved up for a down payment before he spent much time looking for a home. Johnny thought that he would go ahead and at least talk to a lender about the farm he was looking at.

Since I own a mortgage company, I knew what I was talking about when I told him that he was wasting his time. But he went ahead anyway. What took place next was something that I still shake my head at.

Johnny went in and told the banker his whole story—the car wreck, the house in Georgia, everything. The banker admitted that his credit would not allow a loan on the farm he was wanting, not to mention the lack of any down payment.

Nevertheless, the banker then said, "Johnny, I feel real good about you. I want to do the loan for you. I am not going to use your credit report as a gauge for this loan. Instead, if you can at least get me a letter from your current landlord that states that you are paying your current rent, I am going to do your loan."

As if that was not enough, the banker then said, "Since you have no down payment, I am going to loan you the entire amount you need on the property. Although you do not qualify for our best interest rate, I am going to give you the best rate we have." Then things really got crazy. The banker said, "Since there are a few things that we would like to have fixed on the home before you move in, I am going to give you $5,000 in cash to fix up the house that will not be part of your loan."

The banker knew that Johnny was renting and asked him how long it would be before he was free from his current lease. Johnny said three months. The banker then said, "OK, you can move in now, but the loan payments will not start until your lease runs out, so you won't be paying two payments at once. Oh, and by the way, we filled up the propane tank for you as well, and we will pay the homeowners insurance for you at closing."

When Johnny told me all this, I stood there in shock. At the peak of the sub-prime mortgage crisis, when banks were doing everything possible to avoid risky loans, this bank did something that I have never heard of in all my years of business. A few months later I saw Johnny coming down the road on a blue Ford tractor. I knew that those tractors cost thousands of dollars and I knew that Johnny's business was increasing but not at a level yet to pay cash for a tractor. When I asked him about it, he explained that he needed a tractor and he and his wife had asked specifically for this exact tractor. He then told me that one day at church a woman asked him if he needed a tractor and offered him the one he now had. She said he could pay for it later whenever he had the money. Wow! How specific is the Kingdom of God. Johnny and Candi have continued to prosper, setting a record in my company for the first person to break the $70,000 mark for earnings in one month.

Again, I stood in amazement of the Kingdom producing amazing results in the lives of those who belong to God.

These stories are not out of the ordinary for those who have come to trust in the supernatural power of the Kingdom of God. These stories of faith demonstrate that by trusting in the laws that operate the Kingdom of God you can have a tremendous life! Unlike earthly-ruled kingdoms, whose laws are subject to change depending on who is in power or on the will the people, God's Kingdom is based upon Kingdom laws that never change.

In the earthly realm, we have physical laws that do not change. The law of gravity is a law that affects all of us. It does not pick and choose, nor can anyone neglect its effect. If I said I was going to jump off the Empire State Building, you would know with certainty that my end would be quick, because you understand the law of gravity.

In the same way, if I had told you 1,000 years ago that I was going to light an entire building with a glass bulb, you would have laughed at me. You would have thought that it would not be possible, but today we take the law of electricity for granted.

When we use electricity, we just assume it's going to work. So strong is the assumption that electricity is always available, that if a particular appliance doesn't turn on we don't call the power company and say, "Hey, look, I really need this power on today. Could you please turn it on?" And we don't begin to beg with tears trying to convince the power company to help us with the problem. But that is how a lot of Christians act with God. Of course, if we tried that with the power company, they would just laugh at us and say, "Sorry, pal. The power's on here. The problem must be on your end."

Because you understand the laws of electricity, your first thought would be to check the switch or the plug-in. You would realize the availability of power is not the problem. The connection to that power is where the problem lies.

In the same way, an airplane would be viewed as a miracle to people living 2,000 years ago. If they were to see the jumbo jets that are capable of carrying more than a million pounds flying in the sky at 700 miles per hour, they would say, "That's a miracle!" But it wouldn't be. It would really just be the law of lift operating the same way it does for anyone who applies it at any time.

We have become accustomed to the laws of physics, and our lives depend upon them on a daily basis. In a similar way, we have to renew our minds to how the Kingdom operates. As we learn and gain trust in the laws that govern God's Kingdom, fear is replaced with confidence.

Notice how Romans 8:2 refers to these laws. It says, *"Because through Christ Jesus the law of the spirit of life set me free from the law of sin and death."* These laws never change. And this is great news! It offers us hope that we can overcome the destructive lifestyle of debt and lack that affects us in the earthly realm by electing to live under Christ's rule in His Kingdom and learning how the Kingdom works.

It is so incredibly simple that it is easy to overlook.

Wow! Just like the airplane that overcame the pull of the earth's force, Romans says we can walk in the law of the spirit of life. In the operation of the law of the spirit of life, we find access to the inheritance we have as children of God and we find our provision.

It is important to remember that to operate most effectively in the Kingdom of God, we must continually renew our minds with the Word of God and trust in its provision for our lives. The more we come to know and fully understand God's Kingdom, the more fear is removed from our lives and is replaced with confidence.

chapter 7

the power of **the kingdom**

A verse in Scripture that has completely changed my financial life is Proverbs 10:22. It tells us: *"The blessing of the Lord brings wealth, and He adds no trouble to it."* I could probably fill a whole book just with the things God has used Proverbs 10:22 to teach me over the years. But I want to at least explain it enough for you to follow it and step into the blessing of it.

To really understand Proverbs 10:22, we must first go back to Genesis to take a look at Adam. We need to see how God intended man to live in the beginning.

I think you would agree that when Adam was created he didn't fear anything. In fact, the concept of worry and fear were totally absent from his existence. If he had need of provision, he simply gathered it while in the Garden. Of course, if you're familiar with the story, you know something happened to change all that.

Through Adam's own rebellion, he gave away the access he had to the Kingdom of God. He was kicked out of the Garden. In Genesis 3:17-19 we find these words regarding his future:

> *...Cursed is the ground because of you; through painful toil you will eat of it all the days of your life. It will produce thorns and thistles for you, and you will eat the plants of the field. By the sweat of your brow you will eat your food....*

Here we see that Adam became a survivalist. Only by his own painful toil and sweat would he acquire anything.

Today we all view life with Adam's fallen, survivalist mentality. I can prove that claim by asking you this question: If you knew you absolutely *had* to get out of debt and pay your house off, wouldn't you immediately begin to plan on working more hours, picking up another job or two, sending the wife to work, etc., etc.? In other words, your solution would totally involve more laboring, painful toil, and more sweating. Why? Because that's the system you've been raised under. I call it the "earth-curse system." ("Cursed is the earth because of you..." see Gen. 3:17).)

Since the day Adam sinned, humankind has been laboring under the heavy weight of the need to find provision. That's why the lottery is such a tempting lure. We're all tired of running and sweating and the painful toil to find our provision on a daily basis. That's why gambling is a lure too. It's money with no labor attached.

Let's take a fresh look at Proverbs 10:22 in the New King James version in the light of what we've seen in Genesis 3:

> *The blessing of the Lord brings wealth, and He adds no sorrow with it.*

The Hebrew word translated *sorrow* here refers to hard labor, so we could read that Scripture this way: "The blessing of the Lord brings wealth, and He adds no hard labor with it." Of course, this is referring to the earth curse that came on the earth through Adam.

You see, as this verse suggests, God has a new system—one that is not dependent upon your ability to run faster or to toil longer with pain and sweat. Understanding this new Kingdom system is a key to your financial freedom.

Jesus mentions the earth-curse mentality in a parable found in chapter 12 of Luke. Jesus said:

> *The ground of a certain rich man produced a good crop. He thought to himself, "What shall I do? I have no place to store my crops." Then he said, "This is what I'll do. I will tear down my barns and build bigger ones, and there I will store all my grain and my goods. And I'll say to myself, 'You have plenty of good things laid up for many years. Take life easy; eat, drink and be merry'"* (Luke 12:16-19).

Do you see the natural man's thought process here? He thought he finally had enough money saved up to be able to find rest. This is the mentality of natural man: "If I could just become a millionaire, if I could just get enough money saved, then I would have rest and peace."

When Adam lost the provision of God, God gave Adam a picture of what was one day going to be restored to man. It was called the Sabbath. On the Sabbath, man was not allowed to work, or in other words, sweat. God provided for him. The Sabbath was a picture of the restoration of provision for humankind that Jesus was going to make possible.

Hebrews 4:9 refers to this very thing. It says, *"There remains, then, a Sabbath-rest for the people of God."* Could that be true? Is there really a system that we can tap into that allows us to walk above this earth-cursed system of poverty and lack? Yes. Absolutely! But it does take a new way of thinking *and* the help of the Holy Spirit to understand it.

Jesus was constantly demonstrating this new Kingdom to His disciples. For example, we find an interesting story in Mark chapter 6 where Jesus was faced with a multitude of hungry people and had nothing to feed them.

> *By this time it was late in the day, so His disciples came to Him. "This is a remote place," they said, "and it's already very late. Send the people away so they can go to the surrounding countryside and villages and buy themselves something to eat." But He answered, "You give them something to eat." They said to Him, "That would take eight months of a man's wages..."* (Mark 6:35-37).

I want you to notice what they said to Jesus. They could only answer according to the knowledge of the system they had. When pressed with a shortage of provision, they equated it to labor ("eight months' wages").

We could say it in another way. They were basically saying, "Jesus, this is impossible."

When you're facing your financial situation, you may view the problem the same, labor-oriented way. You may think, "I can't run any faster. I can't do any more." That's not the key to your deliverance. The key is learning to tap into the Kingdom of God.

In the situation above, Jesus explained to the disciples the steps they were to take to bring the outcome they needed. The result? They fed 5,000 "men," or very likely 20,000 people counting women and children—and still had 12 baskets of fish and bread left over.

Here we have a clear demonstration of the Kingdom of God as compared to the earth-curse system based solely upon labor, sweat, and toil. The good news is we get to choose which system we live and operate under. Drenda and I have done it, and we've helped countless other couples make the transition as well.

For example, I had a man meet me one day in Canada. He had heard me on television discussing the Kingdom of God. On that day he was so discouraged that he told his wife to go on to church without him. His business was falling further and further behind every month, and he was losing hope. When he saw me on television he said that my story caused hope to return, and he immediately called and ordered my CD series called "Your Financial Revolution." He said the spiritual concepts that I explained on the CDs were so different that he listened to them over and over again. In fact, his wife told me that they literally had my CDs playing 24 hours a day for a month. They were just so desperate and they needed answers. ("Your Financial Revolution" and other proven resources are available for purchase online at FaithLifeNow.com.)

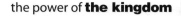

Finally, after listening to my CDs for a month, they felt that they had faith to launch out trusting the Kingdom of God. They decided to start with something small, so they prayed the prayer of faith in agreement as they sowed a small financial gift into the Kingdom of God believing for a vacuum cleaner.

They said that they gave to Faith Life Now, the television ministry that Drenda and I have, because it was through that vehicle they had heard about God's Kingdom principles. A few days later the wife's mother called and asked if they needed a vacuum cleaner. It seems that she had a new one she had never used and just wondered if they needed it. The wife told me that she had never mentioned to her mother that she needed a vacuum before this. They were encouraged by these events and decided that they would believe God for five new clients for their bookkeeping business in the next 30 days.

Again they prayed and released finances into the Kingdom of God believing that they had received these five new clients. In the next 30 days, they did indeed have five new clients. Now they were really encouraged and decided to believe God for something really big. They wanted to believe God that their business would increase to a $10,000 level of cash flow the next month.

At this point their business was running about $5,000 a month. Again they prayed, but this time the husband decided to up their giving as they reached for something this big. Sure enough the next month they did $10,000 in business. When I met them they had been doing over $10,000 a month for nine months straight. You may be wondering, *How did this happen? How did they go from being discouraged and barely paying their bills to having abundance and a new outlook on life?* The answer is simple: they learned how to tap into the Kingdom of God and were diligent in applying its laws.

Mike and Stacey are also a great example of a couple who turned their lives around by tapping into the Kingdom of God. Only a few years ago they were living in an old, worn-out, government-type apartment and were struggling just to buy groceries. Every area of their finances was in trouble.

Mike began to attend our church and began hearing and learning the success principles of the Kingdom of God. Although Mike was in business for himself, the business was not making enough money to provide for his family. Mike comes from a history of weight lifting and was a bouncer in the bar business for years before he became a Christian. When he began attending our church, I put him at the front door where he would help people into the building, greet them, or park their cars.

In that role, Mike began to notice a family that was always crammed into a small car when they came to church. The family of seven could barely squeeze in. Mike had an old van that he was going to sell to get some much-needed cash, but instead he decided to give the van to this family. The family was blessed and thrilled to have the van. And Mike was trusting God for his provision of a new vehicle and the cash he needed.

Now both he and his wife would work out at the gym every day, and one day they saw a poster for a contest. The winner would be the person who could lose the most weight and change their body measurements the most in a certain period of time. Both Mike and Stacey entered the contest. The grand prize was a new car.

I can still remember the day I drove into church and saw Mike near the entrance of the church standing beside his new 2003 limited edition Corvette. Stacey had won the contest. Mike was telling their story to all who would listen. They wisely sold the car to pay their bills, but they were watching the Kingdom of God change their lives.

Mike then began other businesses, and those prospered as well. Still I was shocked when, around the time we launched our television outreach, Mike and Stacey came up to me and said they wanted to sow a gift of $120,000 into the ministry. Actually that year their giving totaled more than $140,000. All of this happened in seven short years.

Just a few years before, this same couple had trouble buying milk and bread, and now they were blessing our ministry with a tremendous check. How they did it was simple. They learned how to tap into the Kingdom of God and were diligent in applying its laws.

To fix the money thing in your life, you're going to have to understand how the laws of God's Kingdom function and the progressive steps associated with these laws. Although space limitations don't allow exploring them all in detail in this book, I will lay out at least some basics that you can begin to apply in your finances.

To see these principles, we'll be going back to the story of Jesus feeding the 5,000. But before we do that, I want to take you forward in His life just a bit and pick up some insights in the story we find in Mark 8:14-21.

> *The disciples had forgotten to bring bread, except for one loaf they had with them in the boat. "Be careful," Jesus warned them. "Watch out for the yeast of the Pharisees and that of Herod." They discussed this with one another and said, "It is because we have no bread."*
>
> *Aware of their discussion, Jesus asked them: "Why are you talking about having no bread? Do you still not see or understand? Are your hearts hardened? Do you have eyes but fail to see, and ears but fail to hear? And don't you remember? When I broke the five loaves for the five thousand, how many basketfuls of pieces did you pick up?" "Twelve," they replied. "And when I broke the seven*

loaves for the four thousand, how many basketfuls of pieces did you pick up?" They answered, "Seven." He said to them, "Do you still not understand?"

Notice that Jesus was bringing to their attention and remembrance a story of provision—abundant provision. He pointed them back to two instances of miraculous provision. Jesus was saying, "Don't you remember?"

Now, let's look back at what Jesus was telling them to remember.

First we need to realize that there were thousands of people in lack at that moment. If you were asked to feed 20,000 people, and you had nothing, you'd have to agree that would be a sizeable task. I doubt your financial situation is that intimidating at this moment. But even if it is, we have a clear illustration in the Bible that shows the Kingdom of God is able to meet the need.

Jesus said, "Remember," so we're going to have to dissect the incident of the feeding of that massive crowd. First of all, when faced with the need, what did Jesus do? Let's carefully note each of these steps.

Step Number One—He said there was an answer that was available outside of the normal earth-curse mentality of labor, which as the disciples pointed out, required eight months' wages. Put another way, you could say their only natural answer was to slave and work for it, and that process would have been way too slow to meet the need in this situation.

Jesus then said, "What do you have?"

This is the first step in operating by Kingdom laws. Jesus identified something that they currently had that could be put under the government of God. Once that asset was transferred to God's domain, He would then have legal access to multiply or effect change with it. Let me illustrate.

Jesus asked, "What do you have?" and they came back with the answer, "Five loaves and two fish." Now, in the natural mind "five loaves and two fish" is not a valid answer to the question, "What are we going to feed these 20,000 hungry people with?" It's not a solution to the problem. That's barely a lunch for one. But Jesus said something that we need to catch. He said, "First, bring it to Me." They did so, and the Bible says He blessed it.

The word *blessed* means to separate or to consecrate. What was He separating the bread from? Well, legally, remember we're talking about a Kingdom. He was separating the bread from the legal dominion of men and placing it under the legal dominion of the government of God. Then He gave it back to them, but they received it back from Him without realizing that the bread was now in a new Kingdom, under a new jurisdiction of law. Then and only then was the bread able to multiply for the people.

So when you have need in the area of provision, step number one is: Find something of what you have need of and sow it into the Kingdom. Jesus taught continually about giving in this way. For example, Luke 6:38 says:

> *Give, and it will be given to you. A good measure, pressed down, shaken together and running over, will be poured into your lap. For with the measure you use, it will be measured to you.*

Step Number Two—The second principle that we need to follow in this story is bringing what we have need of under the dominion of the Kingdom of God, just like Jesus did.

You may ask, "How do I do that?" Well, the Bible is clear on this. It says in Philippians 4:6:

> *Be anxious for nothing, but in everything by prayer* (words) *and supplication, with thanksgiving, let your requests be made known*

to God; and the peace of God, which surpasses all understanding, will guard your hearts and minds through Christ Jesus.

You simply do what Jesus did. You lay your hands on your gift, and you speak over it. You pray and release it into the Kingdom of God.

Let's review. Step number one: "Identify what we have need of." Step number two: "Release it into the Kingdom of God with words."

Step Number Three—We must be sensitive to the plan of the Holy Spirit. Why is this? Because money is not in Heaven. If you ask God for money, He cannot bring it to you because money is in the marketplace. What the Holy Spirit can do, however, once you give Him the care of your provision, is show you where it's at. By giving you an idea, a plan, a direction, a concept, He can show you how to capture what you have need of. In this case, Jesus gave them a plan. "Have the people sit down in groups," He said, "and begin to pass out the bread."

Step Number Four—Once the plan has been made known to you, act on it quickly. In other words, if you receive a direction from the Holy Spirit, don't just sit and think about it. Get up and do it.

A lot of people receive ideas from the Holy Spirit but procrastinate in getting them done. To illustrate this, let me show you another story in the Bible where Peter was asking Jesus about taxes that He had to pay.

Jesus said to him, "Go catch a fish, and in its mouth you'll find a gold coin" (see Matt. 17:27). This was an illustration of how the Kingdom of God met Peter's need. But what would happen if Peter had said, "I think I'll wait awhile. I'll wait a month before I go catch that fish." What would have happened to the gold coin? He would have missed it.

So the fourth principle is, once the Holy Spirit gives you revelation of the answer and the direction, you must act quickly and seize it. One reason quick action is vital is that once the plan is revealed to you, many times the enemy also sees it.

We can ask this question regarding the gold coin in the fish's mouth. Why did Jesus tell Peter to catch a fish with a gold coin in its mouth? Why didn't He tell Peter to go down to the street and pick up a coin off the road or someplace more obvious? The reason is simple: the gold coin was hidden from Peter for Peter. The gold coin was hidden from the enemies of God for Peter's benefit. At the moment of need, it was revealed by the Holy Spirit.

As God brings you a plan—as it's revealed to you—the enemy also begins to pick up on it. That is why, many times, God does not give you the entire picture of your answer until the moment of harvest, because if He did, you may begin to blab about it. The enemy then picks up on that and brings interference against the plan of God.

Step Number Five—The fifth principle of your deliverance is, once the plan is made known, and you understand the urgency of seizing that moment, you must gather the fragments. This means that, by revelation of the Holy Spirit, God is going to point out seemingly little things that are typically overlooked.

For instance, when the disciples fed all of the people on that hillside that day, the Bible says they were all satisfied. Then Jesus said this: "Go pick up the fragments, lest anything be wasted." And they picked up 12 basketfuls of pieces (see Matt. 14:20; Mark 6:43; 8:19; Luke 9:17; John 6:13).

We'll have to agree that feeding the 20,000 by itself was quite a feat for the Kingdom of God compared to the natural way of doing things. But that wasn't all that Jesus wanted to see happen there. So as we step into the Kingdom of God in the area of our provision, we follow the plan of God; we take and seize it quickly once we know about it. But there is more to it than that.

God doesn't just want us to have our needs met; He also wants us to walk in overflow. He wants us to walk in abundance so we can help others and demonstrate His Kingdom to those who are in need.

This comes about by way of the fragments. In a sense, the coin that Peter caught was a fragment. Someone had lost it. The fragments on the hillside, after Jesus fed the 20,000 people, were leftovers. The people didn't really think they had value, but by gathering the fragments and being sensitive to the Holy Spirit, they had 12 baskets left over.

The business that God led me to start many years ago was basically to help people get out of debt and find money (fragments). The basic theme of this whole book is helping find the fragments that are the key to your financial future. A multiplied overflow comes about by direction of the Holy Spirit through finding small pieces that are typically overlooked.

Let me say again, winning in life financially not only requires spiritual laws and understanding the Kingdom, but it also requires understanding the natural laws and obtaining wisdom in the affairs of life. My life was changed by applying the Kingdom of God to my situation.

I remember the night the Lord gave me the dream to start my business. It didn't make sense to me. I was a poster child for doing everything wrong financially. For God to give me a business in the area of finances just didn't make sense. But as we followed His plan and were quick to act on it, those same businesses, which we now own, produce millions of dollars a year in gross revenue.

Just like Mike and Stacey being broke and now being able to give away hundreds of thousands of dollars, like my friends in Canada who saw their business changed, and like Don catching his dream, God wants you to win in life also.

For more information about the Kingdom of God and understanding how it operates, you can go to my Web site at *FaithLifeNow.com* for more resources.

On the pages that follow, I'm going to help you find the fragments of your finances. I'm going to help you see the potential that you have by helping you find money. Then before I'm finished, we're going to put it all together and help you develop a plan to be debt free in less than seven years, including your mortgage. It's an exciting journey.

I'll close this chapter with the words of Jesus in Luke 4 at the beginning of His ministry. Jesus' very first words were about finances. He was reading the scroll of Isaiah out of chapter 61, which contains these words:

> *The Spirit of the Lord is on Me, because He has anointed Me to preach good news to the poor...* (Luke 4:18).

Once you begin to understand the Kingdom of God and the potential and provision within it, my friend, you're going to find that it is indeed "Good News."

fixing the **money thing**

the fix

chapter 8

my five
get-out-of-debt rules

When Drenda and I started our company many years ago, one of the first things we decided was that we needed to give people a simple outline of the things they would need to do to get out of debt. With some time, effort, and thought, we eventually condensed our advice down to five basic, simple rules people would need to master to change their financial future. They have worked for countless others, and they will work for you.

RULE #1: We based the first one on Matthew 6:33: *"But seek first His kingdom and His righteousness, and all these things will be given to you as well."* In this Scripture, Jesus again is contrasting two kingdoms, and telling us that if we would seek *His* Kingdom—if we would understand or take the time to seek knowledge regarding His Kingdom and understand how it works—then we will understand how to access it and walk in it.

It's just as if I dropped you out of an airplane into a foreign nation. Your first objective would be to figure out how that country's system operated so you could find food to eat and acquire shelter. Well, the fact is, you *have* been dropped into a new Kingdom with different rules of operation.

In the same way, when we're born again we're born again into a new Kingdom that we don't understand. We must diligently seek knowledge and understanding through God's Word and revelation of how this Kingdom operates. In so doing, we will find the ability to tap into the inheritance that we have received as citizens of that country.

Second Peter 1:3 says, *"His divine power has given us everything we need for life and godliness..."* or we could say "righteousness." How? "*...through our knowledge of Him who called us by His own glory and goodness."* We have an inheritance that includes everything that we need to live as God designed humankind to live—physically and spiritually. This takes some diligent effort to understand and an investment of time in renewing your mind to the new Kingdom.

This is why Romans 12:2 says,

> *"Do not conform any longer to the pattern of this world, but be transformed by the renewing of your mind. Then you will be able to test and approve what God's will is—His good, pleasing and perfect will."*

Only by renewing our minds will we be able to grasp the different concepts and possibilities that exist in the Kingdom of God.

The Bible says not to be conformed any longer to the *pattern* of this world, referring to the values and thought processes of the worldly culture. If you are a seamstress who used the same pattern and sowed many, many dresses from that same pattern, you would be foolish to expect a different outcome because the outcome is based upon the pattern. What God is saying here is that if you're going to transform your life, you need to learn a different way of thinking than the one you were taught in the earth-cursed system. This new thinking process will only come about by renewing your mind to God's thoughts, which are the Word of God.

I like to tell people that in the Kingdom of God the supernatural is natural. Essentially, the laws of the Kingdom never change. They're as sure as the physical laws that govern this realm. But people who don't understand a set of laws can never gain confidence in them.

For instance, an airplane flying above the earth is using the law of lift in its flight. It's superseding the law of gravity. As I pointed out in the previous chapter, if you do not understand the law of lift, you would say that it's a miracle. It does indeed appear miraculous, but it's not really. It's actually operating consistently and predictably with laws that can be defined, written down, studied, and used by anyone who will apply them.

So in the same way, for someone's life to change financially, he or she must take the time to study, write down, dissect, and understand the function of the laws that govern the Kingdom of God, specifically in the area of finances. In that way, and only through that way, will they begin to grasp and change their thought patterns, which then change their actions, which will in turn change their lives.

RULE #2: Stop using debt. It sounds simple, but it's the first thing the Lord taught me in prayer on that pivotal day I finally came to the end of myself. It was the day the Lord said, "Gary, you trust in debt more than you trust in My Kingdom." It was painful to hear, but it was true.

The debt system is the one almost all of us were raised in. And remember, our first objective is to renew our minds to a new Kingdom system. But to walk in God's system, we must turn away from the old system that we trusted in. Why? Because we will tend to operate within the system that we *most trust* to meet our needs. Unless we decisively and completely turn our backs on the debt system, we will fall back to using it in times of pressure.

A couple of things are important to understand when turning away from debt. In other words, there are some principles you need to enact in your life to protect yourself against debt.

For one, you must live below your income level. Make sure that you can see your budget, see what you're spending, and make wise choices in purchases that do not take you above your income level. Also, begin to set goals for saving. In other words, do you want a newer car? Then save money for that car and pay cash for it. Save money for a down payment on your house. Have financial goals that you are reaching.

I found that it's much easier to spend debt money than it is to spend real cash. For instance, it's much easier to go into a car lot and just walk away with a new car after writing out a small down payment check of, say $200, than it would be to walk in and write a check out for the $60,000 purchase price of that car. Why? Because the value of the $60,000 in your hands seems so much greater than the debt payment that you just committed to.

Another thing we tell our clients is: "Wait. They will still make that item when you're really ready." Don't be pressured into making an impulsive decision to buy something because you think that somehow you'll never have a chance to purchase it again. They will still be making it when you have the cash, and you will enjoy it so much more when you buy it that way.

This principle was so ingrained in my kids while growing up that as we would drive down the road and they would see a really nice car, they would make this statement: "Dad, would you like that car if there were no payments with it?" They understood Dad's objective. Your whole family should understand the objective to stay away from debt.

Remember, freedom is worth more than things. Credit is so available that unless you make a conscious decision to turn your back on the opportunity to use it, it'll be too easy to fall into the seductive trap.

You have to face the reality that your so-called "backup plan" is your real plan. Your safety net is where you have placed your trust and sense of security. That means that carrying your Visa cards around with you, with a line of credit available "in case of emergencies and contingencies," is a way of revealing where your trust lies. Believe me, those cards will be used. Your backup plan, your source of comfort, what you trust in to meet your needs—*you will use.*

RULE #3: This brings me to rule number three, which sounds similar but is actually different. Cut off debt options. This means you must get drastic with steps to protect yourself from ever being forced or tempted to use debt again.

Rule number two centered on your mindset—the mode of thinking and the way you exercise your will in choosing to turn away from debt. Rule number three means acknowledging that you can't trust yourself. Cut off the options. And that means "plastic surgery" is recommended.

You see, everyone will have what I call a *Red Sea experience.* You will remember in the biblical account from the Book of Exodus that the Israelites were crossing the wilderness and came to the Red Sea, with the Egyptian army fast on their trail. It seemed there was no way to cross and escape. The Israelites, seeing the dust storm coming in the distance, grew very fearful, but God made a way of escape supernaturally by splitting the water.

People experience something very similar when they move their trust and allegiance away from the old failed system they have looked to all their lives to meet their needs. There's going to be discomfort, pressure, and fear at first.

Everyone will have a Red Sea experience in which they will be tempted to go back to Egypt—back to bondage and servitude—because it's what they knew. It's what they've trusted in and have found that it (sort of) worked in the past.

Granted, there is some degree of operation and function in that old system. By giving a vendor your Visa card, you do walk away with the goods. You have to agree to be a slave to operate in it, but there is some degree of functionality in that system.

I can assure you that leaving the door open to credit will mean that you will use it, so rule number three: cut up the options. Cancel the credit lines. Cut up the credit cards, and don't give yourself any room for error. Basically, don't make the mistake of trusting yourself in the early days of your decision to turn away from debt.

RULE #4: Giving. This is a powerful rule that people need to walk in. Consistently throughout the New Testament, we see Jesus teaching about giving. Paul did so as well. For example, in Second Corinthians chapter 9 we find these words:

> *Remember this: Whoever sows sparingly will also reap sparingly, and whoever sows generously will also reap generously. Each man should give what he has decided in his heart to give, not reluctantly or under compulsion, for God loves a cheerful giver. And God is able to make all grace abound to you, so that in all things at all times, having all that you need, you will abound in every good work. As it is written: "He has scattered abroad His gifts to the poor; His righteousness endures forever." Now He who supplies seed to the sower and bread for food will also supply and increase your store of seed and will enlarge the harvest of your righteousness. You will be made rich in every way so that you can be generous on every occasion, and through us your generosity will result in thanksgiving to God* (2 Corinthians 9:6-11).

Here Paul is teaching the powerful principle of giving. Giving is the doorway that gives God the opportunity to bless you with opportunities, direction, concepts, and ideas that will propel your life financially. Let me give you a real-world illustration of this truth.

My friend Jerry, a pastor of 30 years, was forced into retirement due to the effects of a stroke. Unable to work, his financial life began to fall apart to the point that one day he found himself thinking about suicide. At a crossroads between life and death, Jerry sat with a loaded .44 pistol in one hand, a Bible in the other. Thankfully, it was at this moment that he came across our television broadcast and heard some words of encouragement about God's Kingdom principles. Jerry wondered, *Could this be true? Could I have been missing these principles* ***all these years?***

Encouraged, Jerry sowed a financial seed out of his need. With no more than $30 left in his pocket, he had an immediate need for $2,000. As an outward sign of his trust in God to meet his needs, Jerry wrote out on a piece of paper that he was believing God to supply the $2,000 by the time he needed it.

A week later an old acquaintance made a surprise visit to Jerry's home. After catching up on each other's lives and reminiscing about the old days, the visitor told Jerry his real motivation for making the visit. "Jerry, the real reason I came by today was that a few days ago I was in prayer, and I felt a very strong urge to bring you this check for two thousand dollars. I was so impressed by the Holy Spirit to do this that I wrote out this piece of paper with the time of day I was actually praying." His friend then pulled out a small piece of paper with the date and time of his prayer.

Jerry was shocked. He reached in his own pocket and pulled out a piece of paper on which he had written the date and time when he had prayed and released his faith. He had also given his financial seed into the Kingdom and believed that he had received $2,000. The two men had written the exact same time on their pieces of paper. Jerry had trusted God, by faith, for the $2,000, and God had spoken to his friend to bring the $2,000.

Giving is a powerful, powerful tool that operates in the Kingdom of God and produces the ability to walk in financial health and freedom. Jerry's life was changed as he began to discover and operate in these laws.

These laws include the tithe and offerings. The tithe (meaning *tenth*) is the 10 percent of our gross income that we give to the Lord. This sanctifies the remaining 90 percent as "off limits" from satan and his plans and schemes.

View the tithe as a fence. If you had a garden and you had animals that were going to eat your produce, you would put up a fence. This fence would keep the rabbits, deer, etc., out of your garden and allow your crops to grow without disruption.

The Bible tells us that the tithe acts in a similar way to a fence. It opens the windows of Heaven and sets a guard around your financial life. But the fence itself does not grow anything. That means the tithe itself doesn't produce increase. Offerings produce increase. The tithe is simply the fence around your money.

What you grow inside the fence you can give away. But as every farmer knows, you need the fence and the seed. Out of the growth of the field, a farmer receives more seed, which will increase his harvest the following year if he plants again.

Here's what I need you to understand. Think of the tithe as a fence and your giving above that as an offering, which you obtain from what you grow inside the fence. When you give those offerings *and* maintain your fence—it produces an even greater increase in your harvest.

The best way to help you understand the principle of the tithe and offerings is to point you to the Book of Haggai. In chapter 1 verse 5-6 we read:

> *Now this is what the Lord Almighty says: "Give careful thought to your ways. You have planted much, but have harvested little. You eat, but never have enough. You drink, but never have your*

> *fill. You put on clothes, but are not warm. You earn wages, only to put them in a purse with holes in it"* (Haggai 1:5-6).

Now does that sound like your life? Or maybe the life of someone you know? Well, in Haggai 1:7 God repeats the warning of verse 5: *"This is what the Lord Almighty says: 'Give careful thought to your ways,'"* which suggests that there was something about the Israelites' ways that was causing the chronic lack in their lives.

God gets more specific in the following verses:

> *"Go up into the mountains and bring down timber and build the house, so that I may take pleasure in it and be honored," says the Lord. "You expected much, but see, it turned out to be little. What you brought home, I blew away. Why?" declares the Lord Almighty. "Because of My house, which remains a ruin, while each of you is busy with his own house. Therefore, because of you the heavens have withheld their dew and the earth its crops. I called for a drought on the fields and the mountains, on the grain, the new wine, the oil and whatever the ground produces, on men and cattle, and on the labor of your hands"* (Haggai 1:8-11).

What issue is God addressing here? Tithing. His people were not tithing. The tithe was to go into the storehouse or God's house. They were not doing that. They were spending the tithe on their own needs and neglecting to bring it to the house of God, and it was in ruins as a result.

According to God's own words in verse 10, they were suffering lack *"…because of you."* He says repeatedly, "Take note of your ways." They were the ones who were cursing their own lives.

God gives a clear picture of the kind of change He is looking for in the very next chapter. After the Israelites began to build the temple and began to put the money toward God in the tithe, as was required in the law, we read:

> *From this day on, from this twenty-fourth day of the ninth month, give careful thought to the day when the foundation of the Lord's temple was laid. Give careful thought: Is there yet any seed left in the barn? Until now, the vine and the fig tree, the pomegranate and the olive tree have not borne fruit. "From this day on I will bless you"* (Haggai 2:18-19).

What happened? They put things in order. They put the tithe in place, which allowed God to bless the work of their hands. Notice that God marked the specific date and time. The minute they changed, God said, "Now I can bless you." Not that God was choosing to withhold His blessing; they were the ones who were not allowing God to bless them. Remember, He said, *"...because of you."*

Clearly, tithing and giving offerings is essential to your financial future.

RULE #5: Develop a written plan to get out of debt. The rest of this book is going to be devoted to helping you develop a plan and locate the money that you'll need to get out of debt. But without understanding the spiritual principles in the laws of the Kingdom, that effort would be useless.

Armed with a written plan that you can frequently refer back to, take direction from, and find comfort in, you will gain confidence that financial freedom is possible for you.

Before we could tackle the "nuts and bolts" of putting this plan into effect, it was vital that you fully understood the spiritual principles that provide the foundation for financial freedom. Be encouraged in knowing that number one, freedom is possible, and number two, your written plan will help you stay on track so you're not distracted by life's pressures and temptations.

Above all, remember, *anyone* can be free.

chapter 9

how to get started

We're going to start our journey to freedom with an assignment. **Number one,** I want you to find out exactly how much you owe. Surprisingly, most people cannot really list and do not have a conscious understanding of who they owe and how much. To start this process, though, we need to know precisely how much you owe and to whom.

So first get a piece of paper out and begin to list your debts. You'll probably have to go to the drawer that you've been stuffing all those bills in, the drawer that you avoid on Monday mornings when it comes time to pay the bills. But this time you're going to face it with courage and pull out everything.

Begin to list the debts—every single one of them—independently on a piece of paper. I want you to list student loans, back taxes, and every single person or entity that you owe money to. This includes family members. We don't want to leave out any debt.

However, we do *not* want to include recurring monthly expenses on this list. Once you have completed this assignment and you see your situation, do not let fear grab your heart, and do not begin to think in terms of hopelessness. You (and your spouse if you're married) need to lay your hands on this stack of bills and ask the Lord for wisdom and for the money to pay these things off. Come into agreement, in the name of Jesus, that you will prevail and you will become free.

Number two, I want you to make a budget—not the pretty kind of budget that you make when you're planning your future—no, I want you to go back three months and analyze what you actually spent. We want to find how you're *really* living. You can use the "present budget" sheet at the end of this chapter.

Most of the families I have met with over the last 25 years begin this process by telling me they have a positive budget with money left over. But once they go back and begin to analyze what they've spent, they're usually surprised to find that their budget is actually negative.

Keep in mind that you're not trying to impress anyone here. You need the facts. You need to know just how negative that budget is before we can move forward and eliminate your debt. We must have a clear picture of reality. We cannot go past this point without understanding exactly where you are in your monthly cash flow.

Number three, after you have written your budget—regardless of whether it's positive or negative—set that aside. Now we must focus on the cash reserve. Most financial planners say you need at least six months' cash set aside as a cash reserve for emergencies.

I would agree with that, but in our company we have families start by just getting $2,000 saved. Sometimes that six months' reserve takes too long and is just too discouraging to start with.

We want to get to working on that debt as soon as possible, but we must put in place a cash reserve that is at least large enough to take care of any major expenses such as tires, a furnace that has to be replaced, or a major car repair.

So we're going to look at the cash reserve situation and list it right alongside your budget. Again, we're trying to get a snapshot of exactly where you are. If you have no cash reserve, do not despair. We will build that. But facing the truth means acknowledging whether we do or do not have any money in savings as a cash reserve.

Number four, we're going to begin the dual tasks of bringing your budget into balance and developing your cash reserve. These are the first two elements in your financial revolution.

Your first steps toward that balanced budget will mean reducing expenses. Begin to take a look at your current expenses and look for all nonessential expenses. List them in the "cash found" sheet at the end of this chapter. We'll look at finding money later, but for now, just see what areas you can change to free up money. This would include things like cable television, satellite television, health club memberships—things that are recurring expenses for things you can live without.

Next, look at what you can sell—that second car, a motorcycle, or the RV. What do you have that can be sold in a garage sale or on eBay? Anything that you're not using in your basement or garage can be converted to cash. This cash can develop your cash reserve, or better yet, even pay off some of your smaller bills, which will in turn free up monthly cash flow.

I remember one consultation that took me into a house where a woman was in tears as she began to tell me the state of her family's finances. Her husband was there with her, but she was obviously the one who carried the burden of paying the bills. We went through their budget and began to look for cash to free up and could find very little.

As I left, I noticed a classic car in the garage, and I asked whose it was. The husband said, "Well, it's my car." I said, "Is it paid for?" He said, "Yes, it's paid for." I said, "How much is it worth?" He said, "$10,000."

I thought it strange that he hadn't mentioned that when I was going through their assets or looking for money. "Well, there's your answer," I said. "You can sell that car and pay off some of your debt, which will free up money for you to begin the process of complete debt elimination."

It was as if someone had hit him in the stomach. With his wife staring at him, tears still coming down her face, he said, "No, I could never sell that car." I stood there shocked at his words. I could see the hopelessness in his wife's eyes as I left. He had missed one of the primary truths about debt elimination—the **"They Still Make It" Rule.** Whatever you're giving up or bypassing now will still be made in that future day when you can pay cash for it without stress or pressure. That husband who couldn't turn loose of that piece of metal didn't have the right priorities. He always could have bought another car once they were free from debt.

So, if you sell something, don't do it in despair and think, *Oh, my life is ruined.* Understand that you will still be able to buy that thing. They'll still make them! Or you can purchase something even better down the road. But right now, freedom is the most important goal.

In many of my clients' cases, once they have done the work of looking at what expenses they could eliminate, and even after selling some expendable assets to free up cash, they still find themselves with a negative budget and no cash reserve established. If you find yourself in the same spot, do not be discouraged because we're going to help you find money.

In fact, that is the next step. I call it financial restructuring and that's the process where we begin to actually look for lost money. But for right now, just make a list of what you found, where your budget currently stands after you have eliminated these expenses, and how much cash you've managed to put aside in your cash reserve.

We'll come back to this money later to see if there's enough there to begin to pay off debt. But for now, let's go on to the next chapter and begin to talk about financial restructuring.

present monthly budget

1. Net Income (after taxes):

Name:______________________ $__________

Name:______________________ $__________

Name:______________________ $__________

Total Net Income: $__________________

2. Expenses:

A. Rent/Mortgage: $__________________

B. Consumer Loans (auto, personal, etc.

Name:______________________ $__________

Name:______________________ $__________

Name:______________________ $__________

Name:______________________ $__________

Name:______________________ $__________

Name:______________________ $__________

Subtotal of B: $__________________

C. Credit Card Payments:

Name:______________________ $__________

Name:______________________ $__________

Name:______________________ $__________

Name:______________________ $__________

Name:______________________ $__________

Name:______________________ $__________

Name:______________________ $__________

Name:______________________ $__________

Subtotal of C: $__________________

D. Insurance:

Auto:________________ $________

Home:________________ $________

Health________________ $________

Life:________________ $________

Subtotal of D: **$**________

E. Living Expenses:

Food: $________

Tithes/Offerings: $________

Utilities: $________

Auto/Gas/Repairs: $________

Medical: $________

Clothing: $________

Entertainment: $________

Misc. (internet, etc.): $________

Childcare: $________

Home Repair/Garden $________

Monthly Investments: $________

Taxes (self-employed): $________

Subtotal of E: **$**________

Total Expenses $________________

Total Budget Surplus $________________

Total Budget Deficit $________________

cash found

source of money found:	amount found:
1. ______________________	$__________
2. ______________________	$__________
3. ______________________	$__________
4. ______________________	$__________
5. ______________________	$__________
6. ______________________	$__________
7. ______________________	$__________
8. ______________________	$__________
9. ______________________	$__________
10. ______________________	$__________
11. ______________________	$__________
12. ______________________	$__________
13. ______________________	$__________
14. ______________________	$__________
15. ______________________	$__________
16. ______________________	$__________
17. ______________________	$__________
18. ______________________	$__________
19. ______________________	$__________
20. ______________________	$__________

total cash found: $______________________

chapter 10

your plan to **the fix**

I want you to take a few minutes to carefully study the details of the plan in the Appendix at the end of this book. Pay particular attention to where money was located and identified by our financial restructuring and how, once it was discovered, it was used to eliminate debts one by one.

You will also notice that as each debt was paid off, we did not release its normal payment back into the budget as free cash. Instead, we redirected it to the next outstanding debt and then repeated this process until all the debt was paid off. This accelerated debt elimination system works to eliminate debt as quickly as possible.

Most of my clients are shocked to see just how fast they can be debt free. In fact, most of the families I've worked with through the years have been able to eliminate all of their debts, including their home mortgage, in five to seven years without changing their income.

As the plan illustrates, I usually recommend paying off very small debts as soon as possible so they can free up some cash quickly. Once those debts are paid off, I encourage my families to pay off their debts in order of their interest rates—those bills with the highest rate first and then the next highest and so on. You will also see that the plan develops a cash reserve as its first priority with the freed-up cash before it moves on to eliminating debt. As was discussed in the last chapter, we aim at $2,000 as the minimum cash reserve we want to first establish.

The power of the plan is really very simple. By locating the financial fragments in your budget—money you didn't realize you were losing unnecessarily or money that was already yours that you didn't realize you had—we find an initial cash flow increase on a monthly basis. This freed-up monthly cash flow then starts the debt elimination process. I think you'll find it exciting to discover that you really do have options about how your money is spent and money that is available to you with just a little bit of effort. When I sit down with a client and show him or her the end result of our financial restructuring, they almost always stare in disbelief, first at the amount of freed-up cash that is available and second at how fast they can really get out of debt.

Don't be concerned if, at this point, you don't know where to begin in locating the missing financial fragments. I will walk you through these steps in the remainder of the book. You will be able to locate some of these fragments yourself as we proceed. In other more complicated matters, you will need help from professionals, auditors, analysts, and companies to help you locate the missing money. Before you start to think that using professionals to help you sounds expensive, let me assure that I have found companies and professionals that do this type of work on a contingency basis only. That means that these types of companies will take a small portion of the money that they find as the fee. If they find no money, there is no fee. I will gladly help you connect with the companies that I have located over the years, and I will also give you tips on how to engage them to find your answers. But for now, let's just focus on the assignments as I give them.

I want you to keep in mind that all the money "found" in the Appendix at the end of this book is dealing with only one client's unique circumstances. The monies you will find through your own audits, reviews, and assessments will be unique to your situation. You may or may not have undiscovered money in every area this client did. And in some categories, you may have more or less than the sample client. The important thing is not to compare your situation to this example, but to use it as a general guide to how the plan works.

Before you are finished with this book, you will have a plan that looks just like this with your numbers in it and the specific steps you need to take to get yourself out of debt. Now if you have finished your list of everyone you owe, let's move on to the exciting part of the process—finding money!

chapter 11

rebuild the **structure**

In our financial restructuring plan, the first thing we always look at is the current debt structure. Interest payments on revolving debt can quickly add up to big amounts of money, and any interest payments we can lower or avoid is that much more money we can apply to our principal amounts which will accelerate our debt elimination progress.

So to begin, let's pull out your assignment from Chapter 9. If by chance you have not finished that assignment let's get that done now. In review, I want you to go to your bill drawer and pull out every debt you have. Even the ones that don't charge you interest, like the loans you made with family members. Every debt should be listed on a piece of paper with the name of the creditor, the amount owed, and the current interest rate on the debt.

Once that is done, we can begin to determine if there are any options or strategies we can use to lower the current interest rates. It is important to note at this point that you *cannot* consolidate yourself out of debt. You may be able to get out of debt *sooner* through consolidation by lowering the interest you're paying *and* by increasing the amount of principal you're paying, but not by simply lumping them all together into one big debt. I hear ads every day that imply consolidation equals eliminating debt. This simply isn't true!

I think those ads are intentionally misleading and offensive. They aim to take advantage of people who are in a great deal of debt and desperate to get out.

One other point I want to make before we get too much further in our debt restructuring discussion is not to get too concerned about amortization schedules. These are schedules that show month-by-month how long it takes to pay off a debt at a specific interest rate or, coming at it from the other direction, what your monthly payments would be if you borrow a specific amount of money at a certain interest rate for a given number of years.

For example, many people are hesitant to refinance their mortgages because they don't want to start over on a 30-year note for their homes. They are worried that by refinancing they will have lengthened the time it will take them to pay off the note. And this would be true if they were to only make the minimum payment each month. But with our accelerated debt elimination plan, you will be paying off your mortgage much faster than the scheduled time period. So for planning purposes, pay no attention to the length of your loans. *Do* pay close attention to what affects the true cost of the loan—the interest rate.

Any decision to change or consolidate any loan you have will be based on this number knowing that we are going to pay much more than the scheduled payment and pay the loan off much faster than planned by the lender. And you will save a ton of money in interest.

The first, and probably largest, of your outstanding debts that I want you to take a close look at is your primary home mortgage. Because first mortgage interest rates have traditionally been the cheapest money you can borrow, you should maximize any options you have there first.

In years past, the rule of thumb regarding **refinancing** was that you needed to be able to lower your mortgage interest rate by at least two points, or 2 percent, before it made financial sense. However, in today's home mortgage market that is no longer the case. Often there are other factors that make refinancing a smart move in your first step toward debt restructuring. In its simplest definition, refinancing a home mortgage involves paying off an existing home mortgage early by taking out a new mortgage at a lower interest rate.

One of the most important things to consider when refinancing your home is how long it will take you to break even considering the monthly savings from the new lower payment compared to the closing costs associated with the refinance. If you take these numbers into consideration, deciding whether or not it makes sense to refinance your home loan usually comes down to determining how long you plan to stay in your home. If you plan to remain in your home for at least the next three years, then that should give you plenty of time for the monthly savings to recoup any costs associated with refinancing.

A second major consideration when deciding if, and with whom, to refinance your home is to shop around for the best interest rates and fees charged. These costs can vary considerably between lenders. One question I'm asked quite often is, "Should I pay more points at closing to bring the interest rate down?" My answer is *no,* this is not necessary. Since we are going to pay off the new loan in about seven years or less, the additional cost is not justified. However, if you were planning to fully pay out the loan as amortized, then paying extra points at closing may save you money.

There is one last detail regarding closing costs that many people overlook. It concerns taxes. In your refinancing process, the current tax law allows you to write off one-thirtieth of the points (which is prepaid interest) you pay at closing on your taxes each year as mortgage interest. Of course, this assumes that you have a 30-year mortgage. Many times this remaining interest deduction from prepaid interest is forgotten from the old mortgage when refinancing, so keep this in mind when preparing your tax returns.

Although there could be many reasons why you would consider refinancing your home mortgage, I would like to identify four of the most popular reasons. These are:

1) to lower your interest rate on your existing loan;
2) to change your loan from a 30-year note to a 15-year one;
3) to change from an adjustable rate mortgage (ARM) to a fixed-rate loan; and
4) to get cash out of your home to pay off high interest rate credit cards.

Let's look a little closer at each of these reasons to determine if one or more of them is reason enough for you to check into making refinancing part of your debt restructuring plan.

The first reason to consider refinancing is also the most common one—to lower your interest rate on your existing first mortgage loan. Refinancing a first is not limited to the original first mortgage, however; it could include combining a second mortgage or consumer debt into the new first. The bottom line is that we want to use the first mortgage to reduce your interest expense on as much debt as we can.

Let me give you an example of how you can determine if refinancing is beneficial. For example, if you are considering refinancing your old mortgage, which is at 7 percent, to a new mortgage at 5.5 percent, you would be saving 1.5 percent a year on the outstanding balance. If your old mortgage had a remaining balance of $100,000 then you would be saving $1,500 a year in interest. If you also included a current second mortgage with a balance of $20,000 at 8 percent into the refinance, you would be saving 2.5 percent a year on that balance as well, which saves you an additional $500 a year in interest.

Adding up all the interest savings that would be available through the new mortgage, we can conclude that the new mortgage would save you $2,000 a year in interest. Next we have to compare this savings with the cost associated with the new loan. This would include all closing costs, appraisal fees, and points. If the total closing costs add up to $2,000, then we can see that refinancing will profit you if you live in your home longer than one year. Along the same lines, if you had credit card debt that you were including in this refinance, you would use the same formula to find your true savings and to determine if you should refinance the mortgage or not.

The second big reason people choose to refinance their homes is to shorten the time to payoff—which usually involves changing from a 30-year to a 15-year mortgage. By doing so it is like you are getting two homes for the price of one! Additionally, interest on a 15-year mortgage loan is usually at least one-eighth of a point less than 30-year loans with other factors being the same.

Let me show you the difference in savings between a 15-year mortgage and a 30-year mortgage on a $150,000 home loan.

At 6.5 percent for 30 years, the total payout would be $341,318, or more than double the amount of the home's value. If you were to take out this same loan for only 15 years at 6.375 percent (one-eighth of a point less than 6.5 percent), you would pay $233,347. That is a savings of $107,971 for just agreeing to a 15-year loan instead of a 30-year one! You would have a slightly higher monthly payment ($348 for this example), but in the long run it'd be well worth it.

Consider this example from Crown Financial Ministries:

> For a typical 30-year mortgage, it will take nearly 24 years to reduce a mortgage to one-half of the amount originally borrowed. Because less than 20 percent of mortgage payments are generally applied to loan payments during the first 15 years (91 percent is paid to interest during the first seven years), homeowners will pay nearly 3-1/2 times the amount originally borrowed before the 30-year loan is paid off. In other words, it will take nearly $500,000 in gross income to

net $300,000 in mortgage payments to pay off a $100,000 mortgage loan.[1]

You can avoid a huge loss by just using a 15-year mortgage instead of a 30-year.

A third reason to consider refinancing is to convert an adjustable rate mortgage (ARM) to a fixed rate.

ARMs are beneficial to lenders because lenders can qualify more people for a mortgage because of the lower entry payment, and the variable interest rate gives the lender a more profitable position. For borrowers, however, an ARM is a home mortgage with interest rates that can be adjusted—usually annually and usually upward. There is usually a 2 percent annual limit on the annual interest rate increase allowed. Many, although not all, ARMs also have a lifetime cap, which limits the total interest increase allowed over the loan. The rate of interest charged is usually tied to a financial index, such as the prime lending rate. As a result, when interest rates rise, the interest rate on your mortgage rises also, sometimes significantly. An increase in the interest rate of your ARM ultimately results in increased expenses for you!

If rates drop, your payment may also decrease, but not necessarily. This is all dependent upon the terms you established when you financed your home.

Frequently, consumers with less than perfect credit scores can only qualify for an ARM. Because they can't get prime rate-based loans, they are given sub-prime rate loans which mean that their personal credit history does not qualify for a prime rate based loan, which offers the best rate. Because the lenders incur more risk with a sub-prime rate borrower they will either offer them a higher fixed interest rate or offer an ARM which is a floating interest rate designed to protect the lender. At the start, borrowers with these types of loans are already at a higher risk credit-wise and frequently lose their homes when the interest rates associated with their ARMs rise and their monthly payments rise higher than they can afford. A lot of the talk you heard back in 2007 about the "sub-prime lending crisis" was all about this very issue.

To buy a home by qualifying (barely) for an ARM is foolish. The safe approach is to either get a fixed-rate mortgage you can qualify for, or an ARM with a good rate and terms you can comfortably manage even if interest rates rise considerably. My advice is to stay away from ARMs from the beginning and, if you currently have one, to look seriously into converting it to a fixed-rate mortgage that you can rely on to remain the same year after year.

A fourth reason people in debt consider refinancing their homes is to pull out some of the cash from the home's equity to pay off outstanding credit card balances. Again, use my earlier example to determine if this move would save you money.

If you do use your first mortgage to pay off debt, never open those credit card accounts, under any circumstances, again—***ever!*** Typically, if someone does this I see the high interest credit card balances climb back up and the consumer finds himself poorer, deeper in debt, and with less equity in his home. Repeat the process a few times and you will find you've used up all the equity in your home and you've pushed the day you own your home free and clear decades into the future.

In conclusion, refinancing your mortgage to pay off credit card balances is a good option if it saves you interest and you are serious about not using consumer debt in the future.

One other restructuring option, which is closely related to using home equity to relieve credit card debt, is using a **second mortgage** instead of a first mortgage to consolidate with.

Unfortunately, I have seen too many families use this option to clean up their various debts only to have it explode in their faces a short time later. This will be the case for you too if you continue to sign up for new credit cards and spend more than you make once your old debts are put into a consolidation loan. If you don't change the habits that got you into debt in the first place, simply putting them all together in one new *giant* loan will not solve your financial problems. In fact, you'll find yourself in worse shape than you were before you took out the second mortgage for the debt consolidation loan.

All that being said, I still like this option because it gives you a tax deduction for all the interest that you *were* paying on all the credit cards (usually up to $100,000) but were unable to deduct. It is also helpful to know that traditionally the underwriting guidelines are less strict than they are for first mortgages, and in the past a borrower could borrow up to 100 percent of their home's value. After the economic crisis most lenders lowered their loan to value guidelines to 80 or 90% of the value of the house.

I don't like to use the typical home equity line of credit that allows the interest rate to float. The unstable rate is a minor problem compared to the fact that borrowers with this type of loan often continue to spend and spend until they have maxed out this line of credit as well. My recommendation is to use a closed-end second mortgage. Although the interest rate is a little higher, you have a fixed interest rate and a fixed payment schedule. I only suggest lines of credit to my clients who have demonstrated some control with their finances. For those who have a history of abusing credit made available to them, I strongly suggest using only closed-end loans.

One other type of second mortgage that was common before the economic meltdown and one I always stayed away from is one that allowed you to borrow money *above* your home's value, up to 125 percent! That's 25 percent *more* than your home is worth!. I always counseled my clients to stay away from these loans because of the problems they can create later if you want to get out of your loan but find you can't.

Before I go on to other debt restructuring options, I need to make mention of another strategy that works well, although it's usually not esteemed as an option by most homeowners, and that is to sell your house and downsize. I don't know what it is, but it seems that people throw common sense to the wind when it comes to their homes. When purchasing a home, many people overlook all the expenses that come with ownership. They think the price of the home is the only expense. But you also have to take into consideration insurance, property taxes, maintenance, utilities, furniture, and more when you buy a home. I have seen this happen many times, including a sad visit with one young couple who called me for help several years ago after being in their home for only one month. After looking over their finances, I had to tell them the bad news—they simply couldn't afford to remain in the house they had just purchased.

I'll tell you what I told them: They will still be making houses in the future when you've put your finances in better order. Get yourself on stable financial ground and then buy a home. Freedom from debt is worth more than anything you can purchase.

Renting is another option that gives you many of the same benefits of owning a home, but with two distinct differences: you don't accumulate equity for all your payments, but you also don't have the large expense of a down payment or the responsibility of maintenance. The landlord is responsible for the property taxes and all repairs. Plus you're not obligated to live there longer than your lease, and you don't have the concerns associated with selling a home.

Throughout my years of working with families facing serious financial problems, many would have been in better financial shape if they had waited to purchase a home and rented while they got their cash reserves built up. Renting and buying both have their advantages and challenges. It is up to you to determine what option is best for you after taking into consideration all the details of your specific case.

If you do own a home, it's always my recommendation to make paying off that mortgage a goal. Ads that encourage people to borrow against the equity in their homes and then invest the money goes against everything I counsel my clients. I'm aware that some financial advisers encourage their clients not to rush to pay off their home mortgages so as to maintain the tax break of the mortgage interest deduction. But if you follow this line of thought, you must realize that you are only getting back 20 to 33 cents for every dollar of interest you pay. If your home is totally paid for, you're not paying *any* interest and you get to keep the whole dollar. Doesn't that make more sense (and cents!)?

Don't be enticed by options for diverting the money you have allocated for your house payment. Having a paid-for home is probably one of the most freeing events in a person's financial life. The sooner you accomplish this goal, the more quickly financial freedom will be yours.

The factors involved bear upon each situation differently, but you get my point. Freedom is worth more than things any day!

There are options other than using your home mortgage as a source of your debt restructuring. One of these is to borrow against your 401(k) savings account. You can usually borrow up to 50 percent of the vested value. The money is paid back to the account as a five-year loan, including the interest, which is usually the prime rate plus one percentage point. The downside is that not only do you repay the loan with after-tax money, but you get taxed again when you withdraw the money in retirement. You also lose the compounded interest you would have received if you left the money alone. If you lose your job while the loan is still outstanding, it usually comes due immediately—within 30-90 days.

If you can't, or don't, pay back the loan in time, it's then considered a withdrawal. If this occurs before age 59½, you have to pay tax on the amount taken out plus a 10 percent penalty. In spite of these possible pitfalls, I have had a lot of clients borrow against their 401(k)s with no problem. If you commit to repaying the loan within the required time period, this can be a workable solution to helping you get your finances in order.

And what about **finance companies?** I don't recommend them to my clients because they usually charge interest rates from 24 to 32 percent. Only once have I had a client successfully solve his debt problems this way and that was because bankruptcy was his only other option. In his case, he was able to consolidate his high-rate credit cards and bring his payment down to an affordable size, which gave him time to make additional money to pay off his debts and look over his options. Generally, finance companies are not an option I support.

Another strategy I have a hard time supporting is the new trend some people are pursuing by obtaining new credit cards that have a zero percent interest rate, in the beginning, and transferring all their debt to these cards. This strategy requires good bookkeeping practices because if you're late on a single payment, the rate goes up to a very high level. In addition, you also have to keep close track of the entry rate time periods so that your balance doesn't suddenly start incurring an unreasonably high interest rate.

It seems to me that if you can go to this much trouble to keep your balances straight on your zero percent credit cards, your time is better spent keeping your finances straight in a simpler, easier-to-understand manner. I know of a couple of people who did this with success. But I also know many people who had good intentions but in the end found themselves with more credit cards and more debt.

One of the newer options for borrowing money is through the Prosper.com Website, which connects people needing to borrow with people willing to loan. The site checks applicants' credit ratings and then posts the amount needed and the maximum interest rate the borrower will pay. Potential lenders then bid on the opportunity to loan all or part of the money and at what interest rate. With a posted time limit, the bidding goes on much like on eBay.

The benefit for those wanting to lend money is that they are able to get a higher rate of return on their money than in a simple savings account at their bank. The benefit for borrowers is that there is more opportunity for those with low credit scores as they are given the chance to tell their story, explaining the circumstances around their need to borrow. The Website monitors all the payments and turns defaults over to collection agencies and reporting bureaus.

Another question that comes up quite often is, **"Should I cash in a retirement account to pay off my debt?"** My first usual response is that you could borrow money cheaper than that. After you pay the 10 percent penalty and pay taxes, you are borrowing money at a rate between 30 and 40 percent. You can find money cheaper than that. However, some of my clients over the years have done this. In dire situations, people have taken the hit and used their retirement money to pay off debt. Cashing out retirement accounts is an option but a very expensive option, and you can get the money cheaper someplace else.

A final direction many people eventually turn to when they are trying to get out of debt is to borrow from family and friends. My advice on this option is simple and straightforward:

Don't.

Almost always, borrowing under these circumstances negatively affects the relationship and rarely brings permanent improvement to the situation.

What is usually needed is a change in *lifestyle,* not cash. There must be a change in the mindset or the work ethic of the borrower for permanent correction to take place. I have personally watched friends lend to other friends to save their home from foreclosure only to have the home go into foreclosure just a few months later. Proverbs 22:7 tells it like it is when it says, *"The rich rule over the poor, and the borrower is servant to the lender."* I have found this true in relationships where someone has borrowed money from the other. When they spot them in the grocery store, they will walk down another aisle to avoid facing them because they do not want to deal with the money they owe them. It makes them feel awkward. As a rule of thumb, if you want to give money to a friend, do that—give it. Never lend it; it is not worth it. My advice is to work out your own money problem and leave your friends and family out of it.

Now if someone wants to *give* you money, free and clear, with no expectation of repayment, that is a different story. Let your family and friends help by praying for you and encouraging you.

Debt restructuring can take many different forms and all of them must be undertaken with caution. It is important to research the option you pursue and be sure to read all contracts and legal documents before agreeing to anything. The last thing you want to happen on your way to becoming debt free is to run up more debt along the way.

If you thoroughly research these different opportunities to help relieve your debt and find the one that best suits you, it can give you just the help you need to get your financial restructuring off to a good start.

fixing the **money thing**

finding money

chapter 12

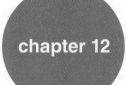

insurance **talk**

"I don't need insurance, Gary. I'm trusting God to take care of me and my family." I've heard numerous variations of that statement throughout my years of working with families to help them get out of debt.

We know that God will take care of all our needs as we trust and obey Him. But often that "obey" part requires being wise with the resources He has given to us. And it means being prudent in our planning for our families.

Proverbs 27:12 speaks of being prepared for the unexpected as it says, *"A prudent man sees evil and hides himself, the naïve proceed and pay the penalty"* (New American Standard Bible). Having insurance is not contrary to believing that God will provide for your needs. It *is* being wise with your money and responsible for your family.

I liken insurance to the foundation of your home. It's frequently unseen and you usually don't give it much thought. It's there doing its job, and that's about all you ever think about it. It's not much to look at. It's usually just a slab of plain, gray concrete. In fact, when most people are deciding what to spend their extra money on when they build a house, people rarely want to invest more in the qualities of the foundation. They would much prefer to spend their money in adding an extra room to the house or some other feature they think they will enjoy and use much more. What they don't realize at the time is the importance of the foundation; that is the base upon which the home is built and holds the entire house in place. So while it isn't especially glamorous, it's extremely important. The same is true with insurance.

Two friends of mine learned the value of insurance the hard way. One was cleaning the second-story windows on his home. He wasn't out doing anything crazy, no extreme sport or anything daredevil like that. He was just getting the cobwebs off the bedroom windows. When the ladder he was standing on slipped, he fell and broke his wrist. The injury wasn't terrible and could have been much worse. The hospital bill, however, could have been terrible to his finances. That broken wrist would have cost my friend $20,000 without insurance. On that particular day he was glad he had insurance.

Another friend didn't think it was important to carry insurance on two vehicles that he wasn't currently driving. He just kept them parked in his driveway. He didn't bother to insure them because he reasoned that they had zero chance of being in an accident. One day he came home from work to find them stolen. He could make no claim to have them replaced because they weren't insured. He simply lost those assets. With that in mind, buy enough insurance to do what it is supposed to do. For example, a $50,000 life insurance policy will do very little to raise your children if something would happen to you. Buy enough to do the job.

The bottom line is that your entire life's work can be wiped out by one event or one lawsuit from an accident. Yes, insurance can cost a lot, but not having insurance often costs much more.

Sadly, many families I deal with don't even know what kind of coverage they have or even where their policies are.

Although insurance may be a boring subject to most people, it's worth looking into. It can be a major contributor to the cash you need in your financial restructuring process. Over the last 25 years in business, I found out that most people have the wrong kind of insurance or are spending too much for what they do have. Many don't realize just how much they can save by making a few minor adjustments to the details of their policies or by replacing their policies altogether with less expensive ones.

My first rule regarding insurance is to set high deductibles on *all* your insurance products. Remember, the higher the deductible, the lower the premium. To do this prudently, you should have a good cash reserve in place, but don't be concerned if you are still working on that. We will help you build that cash reserve as part of your financial restructuring process. So take some time and review all your policies and set high deductibles on your home, health, and auto policies. Besides increasing your deductibles, you should make every effort to begin paying your insurance premiums on an annual basis. What most people don't realize is that by paying monthly or quarterly, the insurance companies add interest to the payment, up to 12 percent a year. Paying your premium annually is like getting a good return on your money and it lowers your premiums.

Another way to save on your insurance costs is to shop around for your coverage. The Internet has made this incredibly easy. You don't have to deal with sales people until you've narrowed your choices down and you're ready to ask questions and make a decision. In most states insurance companies are required to file their rates and plans with their state's insurance commission. Many states have gone a step further and made these rates available directly to the consumer.

In my state of Ohio, I can request a comparison sheet from the state insurance department of all the companies operating within the state and their rates sorted by price and coverage. Benefits and costs vary widely from plan to plan, so it's important to review the details of each.

It's also important to realize that the lowest premium isn't always the cheapest plan. What your insurance covers is just as important as what you have to pay up front.

You should also take into consideration the company's history in paying claims, their financial strength, and their reputation for quality service. It's important to regularly review your insurance policies to make sure you are getting the best deal available at the time and to make adjustments to them as your needs change. The best plan for you is the one with the best price for the benefits you and your family are most likely to use.

Life insurance is an area where I have been able to help thousands of families save money. Let me share a little bit of my history and how I came to learn about the different types of life insurance. I was 18, single, and knew *nothing* about life insurance. I first visited with a salesman at my dad's house. After about an hour of looking at his charts and graphs and numbers, I signed on for a $25,000 whole life insurance policy for about $25 a month. I didn't have any real understanding of what I was buying; it just seemed like the "grown-up" thing to do at the time. It wasn't until five years later, when I came across a little booklet entitled *Life Insurance: The Great National Consumer Dilemma* by Venita Van Caspel that I came to understand how insurance really works and how many people were *losing* thousands of dollars by owning it.[1] Don't get me wrong: insurance is a great product. Some types of insurance, however, can be seriously bad for your financial health.

After reading this booklet and dozens of others as I began to learn more and more about insurance, I came to the conclusion that term life insurance is the ***only*** kind of life insurance to buy. I believed it then and more than 25 years later, it's still what I counsel my clients to purchase. One important note before you begin changing your insurance coverage: under no circumstances should you cancel an existing policy until you have proof of a new policy in your hands.

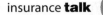

Take a look at the example illustrated in Exhibit A at the end of this chapter. It's a proposal for a **cash value life insurance policy** on a 52-year-old male and will illustrate some of the problems I see with this type of coverage. The annual premium for the policy is $3,224.64, which provides a $250,000 death benefit. Please pay particular attention to the death benefit column on the right side of the page. Notice that even though the cash value is growing inside the policy, the death benefit does not. In fact, in year 31 with $91,000 of the policy owner's own cash in the policy, the proceeds paid out at death are still the same $250,000.

The same company also offers a ten-year term policy that offers the same protection at a lot less money. The same $250,000 death benefit would only cost $498.08 a year for the term policy. The cost difference between the two policies is $2,755.56 a year. The key fact here is that both policies will pay out the same $250,000 upon the death of the insured.

So my question to you is: Would you rather pay $3,224.64 or $469.08 to receive the same check for $250,000? That's obvious. On the other hand, if you were the insurance company, which would you rather *sell,* the $3,224.64 annual premium or the $498.08 annual premium for the *same* $250,000 payout? Again, obvious, except that it's the insurance company that profits, not you!

The supposed difference, as the insurance company likes to point out, is that by buying the more expensive policy (the cash value policy), you are saving money for retirement at the same time you are providing for your family upon your death. The problem with this product is that upon your death the company keeps all of the money that you have saved for retirement and does not pass it on to your spouse but simply pays the death benefit or face value of the policy.

If the insured had just bought the term insurance and saved the difference somewhere else, upon the death of the insured, the spouse would have the $250,000 death benefit *and* the money that had been saved for retirement.

Another disadvantage to the cash value policy is that if you want to access some or all of the money you have been saving inside of the policy, you have to take out a loan against it and pay interest on borrowing your own money! Think how many customers a bank would have if their advertisements stated: "We are not like most banks. If you need money out of your savings accounts we will draw up a loan agreement and charge you interest for taking your money. If you die, we will keep your money and your estate cannot have it. And finally, if you leave it here, it will take three years before any deposits or growth will begin to show up. And by the way, you will earn about 2 percent and your account cannot qualify as an IRA retirement account." I don't think you'd go for that, but millions of people do. After all, banks don't have those "crazy" rules.

So if you currently have policies that are labeled whole life, universal, or variable life, dump them and put the difference in savings or apply that cash toward paying off your debt. Just remember under no circumstances should you cancel an in-force policy before you have a new policy in your hands. You can reach my firm Forward Financial Group for help with this nationwide at 1-800-815-0818.

Throughout all of this discussion about insurance, it's important to keep your eye on the ball. The primary purpose of life insurance is to provide for your dependents upon your death. Period. Usually the amount of insurance you buy should be determined by the ages of your children, your earning potential to your spouse, and your existing debt.

I usually recommend buying ten times your annual salary minus any cash assets you have, but do not include your home as part of the equation. That means that if you have $500,000 in the bank, you wouldn't need a $500,000 life insurance policy. Be sure you realize that even though $250,000 sounds like a large policy when you are younger, in the long run, it would not be nearly enough to cover the cost of raising your children, especially if they are very young and if you include plans to take care of college expenses. A good agent can work with you and help you map out a plan to help your family be taken care of for many years. For your spouse and children, knowing that you've taken care of them financially is some of the best insurance you can provide them and yourself.

Over the years I have seen many families without **health insurance** due to the high cost of owning personal health policies. On the other hand, it's amazing to see what some people are paying for their health insurance. This makes health insurance a prime target in our financial restructuring. Most people have health insurance through their employers. They pay for part of it and the company pays for part of it. The employee benefits from the reduced rates offered to the group rather than paying the high individual premiums.

Usually these plans are the typical group major medical plans with a deductible and a "stop loss" clause that limits the out-of-pocket risk of the insured per calendar year. The cost of any claim is shared 80/20 up to the stop loss point, which is usually $5,000 to $10,000 after the deductible, which is usually $500 to $1,000 a year. Clients who have no group coverage available to them and buy their own health insurance may be paying $500 to $1,200 a month for this type of coverage. Health insurance for the average family will be taking on a whole new look as the major health insurance bill passed Congress in March of 2010. Until those changes and how they will play out with the group insurance offered by employers is better understood in the years ahead, I believe there is a better way.

For my family of seven, we have found a way to avoid these high monthly premiums. We maintain a high deductible health plan with a **Health Savings Account** (HSA) attached. We currently pay $275 a month for our high deductible major medical coverage with a $5,000 deductible. I put pre-tax money into an HSA every month, and those funds can be used for all kinds of medical expenses with no deductible involved. And I'm paying those expenses with pre-tax dollars! Rates vary by age and location as well as between insurers so take the time to do some shopping in your state for the best rate and plan.

There are limits to the amount you can place in your HSA, so check to see which apply to you. I also have a Visa debit card that draws only from my HSA, and I use it whenever anyone in my family goes to the doctor or dentist. Because most routine medical and dental expenses are usually fairly small, we are able to use the HSA to pay these bills. You also don't have to worry about meeting a deductible each time you have a medical or dental expense as long as there's enough money in your HSA to cover the expense.

It's a great feeling to know that the money in my HSA is mine and that if I don't use it all up, it can be applied toward retirement.

I've looked at many types of health policies over many years and having an HSA is my favorite. If your employer doesn't offer one, ask to see if it can be added. If that isn't an option, I have even known of people who ask to be removed from the company-wide insurance plan and given their portion of the company's expenses on their behalf to apply to the insurance of their choice. If you can do this, it will give you the opportunity to manage your health insurance expenses to the greatest advantage for you and your family.

Another type of insurance that people constantly ask me about is **long-term care insurance.** According to Crown Financial Ministries, it is estimated that 40 to 50 percent of Americans over the age of 65 will enter a nursing home sometime during their lifetime. Of these, almost 70 percent will also need to have some type of in-home care. With nursing homes rates currently at $25,000 to $50,000 a year, it wouldn't take many years to wipe out most families' savings. At home, around-the-clock care by licensed medical personnel can run in the hundred of thousands of dollars. If you add these financial worries to the emotional issues of dealing with a sick or elderly person, it's easy to see the benefits of adding long-term care to your policy. However, as I have said with each of the insurance options, it's important to weigh the cost of the policy against your anticipated need for it in the future. There are many long-term care policies on the market. Some are better than others. Take the time to read through several of the options out there before you buy.

Be sure that you understand the wording and the benefits of each policy. Long-term care should be part of your insurance portfolio and could save your spouse or your children thousands of dollars.

Regarding all the other specialty types of insurance available, such as cancer insurance or accidental life insurance, I think they are generally unnecessary. Buy good health insurance and forget the cancer insurance. Buy good life insurance and forget the accidental death protection. Get your "bases covered," but don't buy every type of insurance that comes along. The only additional type you might consider is **disability income insurance,** which provides income if you became seriously sick or injured. This might be especially helpful if you are the sole wage earner, you work in a dangerous job, and you have a family dependent upon you.

Be sure that you have adequate **liability insurance** on your automobiles and your home. Don't settle for the minimum required by law. If you have your own business, always make sure you have good liability insurance and errors and omissions (E&O) insurance to protect you from lawsuits.

Speaking of legal issues, I consider **prepaid legal insurance** to be well worth its cost. Among other things, this type of insurance gives you unlimited access to an attorney by phone to answer any question you may have about buying a car or signing a lease or any legal question you may have. They can even handle domestic questions about where you can legally put your fence or who is liable if your tree damages your neighbor's house. The areas they can assist you in are unlimited and can be of great value financially.

Monthly premiums can be as low as $16 to give you access to professional legal counsel.

I have used Pre-Paid Legal Services Inc. based in Ada, Oklahoma, for this service for the past ten years, and I'm confident they have saved me much more than the premiums have cost. Basic plans include representation during an IRS audit or in a civil lawsuit. I also take advantage of the yearly offering to review and revise my family's wills for only $20. The unlimited toll-free calls to professionals and their free reviews of all my legal documents has helped me tremendously through the years with my legal concerns. I think everyone should own it.

Although owning insurance is not specifically addressed in the Bible, buying insurance to ensure the welfare of your family is a God-honoring act that demonstrates responsibility *for* your family *with* resources that God has trusted you with. When insurance is bought with this frame of mind, it can relieve many of the outside worries of the world and allow us to live in peace.

[redacted] Life Insurance Company
Life Insurance Policy Illustration

Prepared for
[redacted]
Age 52

Flexible Premium Adjustable Life
Executive Universal Life 5

Underwriting Class: Male, Preferred Non-Smoker
Interest and Cost Scenarios:
Guaranteed: 3.50% interest rate, Maximum charges
Illustrated: 5.00% years 1-10, 6.00% years 11-20, 6.15% thereafter, Current charges (The current rate is 5.00%)

Non-guaranteed benefits and values are subject to change and may be more or less favorable than shown. This illustration assumes premiums are paid on the Monthly due date. Values and benefits are as of the end of the policy year and will vary depending upon the amount and timing of the premium payments.

					Guaranteed			Non-Guaranteed Illustrated		
End of Yr	Age	Opt	Annualized Premium Outlay	Type*	Policy Fund	Cash Value	Death Benefit	Policy Fund	Cash Value	Death Benefit
1	53	1	3,224.64	P	1,028	0	250,000	1,711	0	250,000
2	54	1	3,224.64	P	1,917	0	250,000	3,423	0	250,000
3	55	1	3,224.64	P	2,692	0	250,000	5,168	0	250,000
4	56	1	3,224.64	P	3,288	0	250,000	6,946	0	250,000
5	57	1	3,224.64	P	3,700	0	250,000	8,763	1,483	250,000
6	58	1	3,224.64	P	3,919	0	250,000	10,649	3,609	250,000
7	59	1	3,224.64	P	3,877	0	250,000	12,610	5,810	250,000
8	60	1	3,224.64	P	3,562	0	250,000	14,649	8,089	250,000
9	61	1	3,224.64	P	2,929	0	250,000	16,714	10,634	250,000
10	62	1	3,224.64	P	2,547	0	250,000	19,397	13,957	250,000
11	63	1	3,224.64	P	1,719	0	250,000	22,721	18,001	250,000
12	64	1	3,224.64	P	390	0	250,000	26,101	22,341	250,000
13	65	1	3,224.64	P	0	0	250,000	29,517	26,717	250,000
14	66	1	3,224.64	P	0	0	250,000	32,979	31,059	250,000
15	67	1	3,224.64	P	0	0	250,000	35,823	34,863	250,000
16	68	1	3,224.64	P	0	0	0	38,798	38,798	250,000
17	69	1	3,224.64	P	0	0	0	41,780	41,780	250,000
18	70	1	3,224.64	P	0	0	0	44,978	44,978	250,000
19	71	1	3,224.64	P	0	0	0	48,410	48,410	250,000
20	72	1	3,224.64	P	0	0	0	52,092	52,092	250,000
21	73	1	3,224.64	P	0	0	0	55,879	55,879	250,000
22	74	1	3,224.64	P	0	0	0	59,665	59,665	250,000
23	75	1	3,224.64	P	0	0	0	63,440	63,440	250,000
24	76	1	3,224.64	P	0	0	0	67,191	67,191	250,000
25	77	1	3,224.64	P	0	0	0	70,952	70,952	250,000
26	78	1	3,224.64	P	0	0	0	74,737	74,737	250,000
27	79	1	3,224.64	P	0	0	0	78,559	78,559	250,000
28	80	1	3,224.64	P	0	0	0	82,435	82,435	250,000
29	81	1	3,224.64	P	0	0	0	86,340	86,340	250,000
30	82	1	3,224.64	P	0	0	0	90,311	90,311	250,000
31	83	1	3,224.64	P	0	0	0	94,349	94,349	250,000
32	84	1	3,224.64	P	0	0	0	98,399	98,399	250,000
33	85	1	3,224.64	P	0	0	0	102,407	102,407	250,000
34	86	1	3,224.64	P	0	0	0	106,299	106,299	250,000
35	87	1	3,224.64	P	0	0	0	110,091	110,091	250,000
36	88	1	3,224.64	P	0	0	0	113,626	113,626	250,000

This Basic Illustration Is Not A Policy Contract
and is not valid unless all pages are included

SIL124 (5.1) Page 5 of 8

[redacted] Life Insurance Company
One Midland Plaza, Sioux Falls, SD 57193-0001

Prepared for:
[redacted]
Age 53, Nearest Birthday
Male Preferred Plus

Modified Premium Term Life to Expiry Da
Premier 10 Term - Century Series
Policy Form # T083E1 seri

--------------- GUARANTEED ---------------

Age	Year	Maximum Monthly Premium	Maximum Annualized Premium	Death Benefit
53	1	34.50	414.00	250,000
54	2	34.50	414.00	250,000
55	3	34.50	414.00	250,000
56	4	34.50	414.00	250,000
57	5	34.50	414.00	250,000
58	6	34.50	414.00	250,000
59	7	34.50	414.00	250,000
60	8	34.50	414.00	250,000
61	9	34.50	414.00	250,000
62	10	34.50	414.00	250,000
63	11	553.81	6,645.72	250,000
64	12	616.81	7,401.72	250,000
65	13	683.31	8,199.72	250,000
66	14	750.69	9,008.28	250,000
67	15	818.94	9,827.28	250,000
68	16	892.44	10,709.28	250,000
69	17	968.56	11,622.72	250,000
70	18	1,060.88	12,730.56	250,000
71	19	1,164.13	13,969.56	250,000
72	20	1,299.75	15,597.00	250,000
73	21	1,442.81	17,313.72	250,000
74	22	1,593.31	19,119.72	250,000
75	23	1,757.81	21,093.72	250,000
76	24	1,937.19	23,246.28	250,000
77	25	2,145.44	25,745.28	250,000
78	26	2,388.69	28,664.28	250,000
79	27	2,669.56	32,034.72	250,000
80	28	2,975.81	35,709.72	250,000
81	29	3,324.50	39,894.00	250,000
82	30	3,687.63	44,251.56	250,000
83	31	4,079.19	48,950.28	250,000
84	32	4,512.75	54,153.00	250,000
85	33	4,997.06	59,964.72	250,000
86	34	5,533.87	66,406.44	250,000
87	35	6,120.13	73,441.56	250,000
88	36	6,748.38	80,980.56	250,000
89	37	7,411.19	88,934.28	250,000
90	38	8,102.87	97,234.44	250,000
91	39	8,753.44	105,041.28	250,000
92	40	9,431.56	113,178.72	250,000

This Proposal is not a Policy Contract

SIT083E1 Page 2 of

chapter 13

a double take **on taxes**

Guess who said, "The hardest thing in the world to understand is the income tax"? That would be Albert Einstein. Yep, Mr. Theory of Relativity himself. It has to make you wonder how the rest of us are supposed to manage. And the tax code has only gotten more complex in the years since Professor Einstein died.

It's no wonder so many of us have a tough time understanding the many, many details of our federal income tax returns. The IRS itself has admitted that it gave incorrect and insufficient advice 80 percent of the time in the year 2000, and 73% in 2001. In response to this, the IRS countered that it is getting better. In 2009, tax returns prepared by the IRS's own free assistance program were only wrong 41% of the time. Well that error rate should comfort all of us! The bottom line is that the IRS's own inefficiency translates into billions of dollars overpaid in taxes by millions of Americans.[1]

For most people, taxes are the most expensive item they pay each year. In fact, it's usually well into April of each year before Americans reach the point that they stop working for the government and are actually working for themselves. All funds made before that date would, percentage-wise, be owed to the IRS. Because this represents such a large part of our earnings, doesn't it make sense to get a second opinion or additional counsel for how much you turn over to the federal government? We're willing to drive across town to save a few dollars for something on sale, but frequently with taxes we just assume that anyone who prepares and files taxes for us is doing so correctly and getting us the lowest bill legally possible.

Money magazine conducted an ongoing study of tax preparers—one that was done eight times in a ten-year period.[2] Their research showed beyond any doubt how often mistakes can and are being made by tax professionals in preparing income tax returns. In the study, the same client's financial profile was sent to 50 seasoned tax professionals for their review. It was to be used to complete the family's tax return. The table below shows the results from the study.[3]

Yr. of Tax Test	Range of CPA's Amount Due	% Difference in Stated Amount	Range of CPA's Fee's
1987	$7,202-$11,881	165%	$187-$2,500
1988	$12,539-$35,813	286%	$250-$2,200
1989	$9,806-$21,216	216%	$271-$4,000
1990	$6,807-$73,247	1076%	$375-$3,160
1991	$16,219-$46,564	287%	$520-$4,500
1992	$31,846-$74,450	234%	$375-$3,600
1996	$36,322-$94,438	260%	$300-$4,950
1997	$34,240-$68,912	201%	NA

When I saw the results, I could hardly believe it. The results from 1990 are especially shocking. The amount of taxes owed range from $6,807 to $73,247, again, for the same client. That's an incredibly large difference in tax bills. On the one hand, you certainly do want to pay what you owe. On the other hand, how much do you owe? My personal opinion is I want to pay the smallest amount of tax the law will allow. As you can see, there seems to be a lot of confusion finding that number.

That confusion is costing tax payers millions of dollars in overpaid taxes a year. *Money* magazine also did another survey. They sent a hypothetical financial profile to 50 preparers picked at random from the yellow pages in Atlanta, Minneapolis, Philadelphia, Seattle, and San Diego. All 50 preparers were given the same ten questions to answer. The results from this experiment were as shocking as the previous study. Of the 50 preparers, none of them got all ten questions correct and only 34 got at least half of them right.[4] Yet another case for the argument to get a second opinion on your tax return. The response from *Money* magazine at the conclusion of the study said it all:

> The implication for you (the taxpayer) is obvious. Chances are your return is so riddled with errors that even if it's one of the 48% that will be handled by a professional tax preparer, you can figure you are paying 25% too much income tax.[5]

Kevin McCormally of Kiplinger's *Cut Your Taxes* explains the process of recouping some of the money you may have overpaid in the past. He says:

> You have three years to amend a tax error. An amended return is filed on Form 1040X and must be filed within three years of the filing date for the tax year in question. Be sure to use the tax rates for the year of the return you are amending. Send the amended return to the IRS Service Center for the area you now live in, even if the original return was filed elsewhere.[6]

When large returns are at stake, most taxpayers will file amended returns. But some worry that an amended return will trigger an IRS audit. The IRS says this is not so. Most tax experts agree that amended returns do not usually trigger an audit, saying that most changes get no more scrutiny than if you made the claim on the initial return.

The good news about getting help for your tax returns is that you don't have to go from accountant to accountant asking questions and comparing answers. Quite a few companies will review your returns for the past three years for free. The catch is that they work on a commission basis, allowing them to keep a portion of whatever overpaid money they identify, sometimes as much as 40 percent. But the way I see it, the money was "lost" to me already, so anything I get back from one of these reviews is more than I had before.

Another benefit of these companies is that they will guarantee in writing to back up their corrections in a tax audit at no additional charge. They will also work with your accountant to help him/her not repeat the same mistakes in the future. This can save you many, many dollars on future filings. To learn more about these type of companies, go to ForwardFinancialGroup.com. As proof of their services, they claim that six out of ten small business returns are wrong, and that, once corrected, businesses receive an average refund of $6,000 to $10,000 after reviewing three years' worth of returns.

Another huge tax loss area is the yearly tax refund. Many of my clients are elated to receive a tax refund. According to *USA Today* dated March 23, 2006, John Waggoner states that the average tax refund for 2006 was $2,379 and three out of four people would get a refund.[7] Although a tax refund is popular, a tax refund is really a loss. A refund is paid as a result of you overpaying your taxes throughout the year, usually through payroll deduction. The IRS is simply giving you back your overpayment without any interest attached. If you were dealing with a bank, you wouldn't give them your money without expecting to get some interest paid back also. To prevent overpaying your taxes, I generally suggest to my clients to increase the allowances on their W-4 forms. This will in turn reduce the withholding from your paycheck.

People always seem hesitant to adjust this common mistake in fear that they will have to pay at the end of the year when the allowances I'm suggesting they take are larger than their family. I find that people are confusing dependents with allowances. You claim your dependents on your Form 1040 when filing your taxes for the previous year. The W-4 form asks for allowances that would reduce your tax bill for the coming year. Most people only claim themselves, their spouses, and their children as allowances. If you itemize your return, you can also figure in mortgage interest deductions, charitable giving, and child credits. To review a complete W-4 worksheet explaining possible allowances, ask your employer or go to IRS.gov.

I often have clients ask me what to do if they owe back taxes. I always remind them that I am not in the tax consulting business, but I do recommend that their first step should be to talk to the IRS. They offer several options and remedies to help people in this situation. One of the options the IRS does not frequently present is Form 843, which allows you to file for an abatement refund of penalties and interest on back taxes after they are paid. Very few people know of this option and yet it can help you greatly. You have two years to file for the abatement after paying the year in question completely off. If you owe taxes on several past years, you can file a Form 843 each time you pay off interest and penalties for a given year and have the abatement applied to the remaining taxes owed to help pay them off even faster. The form does ask for a reason for the late payment and I recommend being completely honest with your answer. If you didn't have the money at the time, just tell them and turn in the form.

One other very valuable resource for tax information is author Dan Pilla and his many books on dealing with the IRS. He presents the information from a Christian viewpoint in a very helpful manner. His company can be contacted at taxhelponline.com or at 1-800-34-NO-TAX.

As Ben Franklin supposedly said, "There are only two things in life that are certain: death and taxes." If you have a relationship with Jesus Christ, the eternity part of that equation holds no fear.

If death can't scare us, why should our taxes?

chapter 14

strategies for **business**

As I travel and teach people about the Kingdom of God and how it works, I'm always amazed at how many Christians truly believe God is responsible for bringing them money. They either believe that God will just step in and take care of the money situation or, if they give into the Kingdom, all they have to do then is to sit back and wait for God to bring it to them. God does not have any money in Heaven; He doesn't need it there! Money is on the earth and in the hands of men.

Think back to the story of Jesus being tempted by satan in Luke 4:6-7. In this story, satan led Jesus up to a high place overlooking all the kingdoms of the world and said, *"...I will give You all their authority and splendor, for it has been given to me, and I can give it to anyone I want to. So if You worship me, it will all be Your"* (Luke 4:6-7). The splendor he was referring to was the wealth of the nations, or the kingdoms of earth, and he was claiming them to be under his dominion.

Money, just by its very nature, is a product of a kingdom, an earthly kingdom because money is not of Heaven, only of earth. Because of this, God cannot just take it from one person and give it to someone else. That would be stealing and certainly not something God would be a part of. If this is the case, how does God allow believers to receive money? A good example of this is in Second Kings 4:1-7 as it says:

> *The wife of a man from the company of the prophets cried out to Elisha, "Your servant my husband is dead, and you know that he revered the Lord. But now his creditor is coming to take my two boys as his slaves." Elisha replied to her, "How can I help you? Tell me, what do you have in your house?"*
>
> *"Your servant has nothing there at all," she said, "except a little oil." Elisha said, "Go around and ask all your neighbors for empty jars. Don't ask for just a few. Then go inside and shut the door behind you and your sons. Pour oil into all the jars, and as each is filled, put it to one side." She left him and afterward shut the door behind her and her sons. They brought the jars to her and she kept pouring. When all the jars were full, she said to her son, "Bring me another one."*
>
> *But he replied, "There is not a jar left." Then the oil stopped flowing. She went and told the man of God, and he said, "Go, sell the oil and pay your debts. You and your sons can live on what is left."*

In the story, the woman desperately needed money. The Lord met her need by multiplying something she already had that could then be sold in the marketplace. In a sense, **God put her in business,** the "oil" business, so she could have money to live on and support her sons.

God used this same concept to bring money into my household when I was broke many years ago. He gave me a dream one night that led me to go into business and help families get out of debt. Ever since then, I have loved owning a business. Both people and money are in the marketplace. It's where all the action is! Because of my experiences, I'm always encouraging others to go into business as well. So in regard to getting money, always remember that since money is not in Heaven, God helps us capture it here on earth through ideas, concepts, and direction to our lives in the business world.

With more than 28 years in business for myself, I've learned many things along the way—some the hard and tedious way, others quickly and easily. I hope by sharing my experiences and the wisdom I've gained through the years, I can help you succeed faster and better. What follows are what I consider to be some of the most valuable lessons I've learned.

Hire an Assistant

When my business was just starting, my wife Drenda and I did it *all!* We answered the phones, met with clients, processed orders, and took care of the bookkeeping. Believe me, this took an extraordinary amount of time. I finally came to realize that all this time-consuming office work did not pay the bills. Sure, it was necessary to keep things running smoothly, but the only thing that generated money for me was to meet with clients. I was busy in the beginning but busy doing the "wrong" things. After I figured my time to be worth $150-$200 per hour when I was meeting with clients, it didn't take me long to see that I was "losing" money by shuffling papers and doing office work at what could be an $10-per-hour job! My advice: focus on what you do that produces income for the business and hire everything else out.

Hire a Payroll Processing Company

Again, in the early days of my business, I often had to stop "producing" money and take time out to figure my quarterly payroll reports, file the W-3 report, calculate and print W-2 forms, and pay any taxes that were due. Because I was trying to do so many things at one time, several times I was even late on making a tax payment, which ended up costing me a penalty. I also had to put a lot of time and figuring into making sure I had enough money in the bank to pay my quarterly tax bills. This seems to be a common problem for companies in their early years as business owners just get behind on their taxes and the debt continues to grow.

Because of this, I strongly recommend hiring a payroll processing company to take care of all these very detailed reports and payments. Having done it myself in the beginning and then moving on to hiring a company to handle it for me, I will *never* again attempt to take care of this job myself. I've come to realize that through a payroll company's efficiency and attention to detail, I end up saving lots of dollars in the end. You can call my company Forward Financial Group at 1-800-815-0818 for information about the lowest price payroll processing firm I found.

Use a Courier

Time spent running business errands is time spent *not* producing income. Besides, the hassle of city traffic was always something I tried to stay away from if I could. As a result I began using a courier to pick things up at my office and drop them off on the other side of town, usually for only $25 a trip. I also began ordering my business supplies online and having them delivered. I used a postage meter at the office so I could send things out directly without having to go to the post office. Whatever your errands are for your business, ask yourself, "Who can I find to do this task for me?" This will free you up to do what is most beneficial for your business—make money.

Get the Structure Right

When I was first in business, I operated as a sole proprietorship. This worked well for a while, but eventually my accountant told me I needed to change the structure of my business. He advised me to incorporate the business and begin operating as an "S" corporation. Because I knew next to nothing about the different business structures, he explained to me why becoming an "S" corporation would be best for me and showed me that, with a few simple changes, I could save $10,000 a year in taxes. Since then LLCs and Limited Partnerships have also become very popular business models, which you will have to explore in regard to your needs. Since those early days I have been a firm believer in getting sound business advice from a professional. Because they deal with these things all the time, they know what is best suited for your business and how to protect your personal assets from potential lawsuits. It's advice that is worth every bit of what it costs.

Use an Attorney to Review All Legal Papers

It's hard to imagine one of your employees ever actually suing you, but sometimes as employees see the company making a fair amount of money, they see it as an opportunity for them to get a share of it through a lawsuit. They sometimes even begin to question how loving and generous you are if they don't receive what they consider to be fair pay. With this being said, you have to have all of your employment contracts and handbooks reviewed legally. If you don't even have an employee handbook right now, take care of it immediately! Include in it job descriptions for every position.

Also, before signing any lease or business contract, have it reviewed by an attorney for his or her opinion. Years ago we were about to sign a contract with people we considered friends for some expansion work on our business. As we had done business with them in the past, we weren't too concerned about the terms of the contracts when the contracts were small—around $3,000 to $4,000. But this new contract would cost closer to $100,000 before it was all done. Once our friends saw the amount of the contract, they began acting strange and asked us to promise to give them credit for their work should we be asked about it. They saw the size of the job as giving them considerably more exposure and wanted to control more of the product details.

When our attorney reviewed the terms, he advised us in no uncertain terms not to sign the contract. He went so far as to say that by signing this agreement, we would be violating our financial integrity to our board, and that was something we didn't want any part of. The sad fallout that resulted from us declining to accept the contract was that our "friends" attempted to sue us. Eventually we resolved the dispute with them, but we were very thankful our attorney kept us from putting our business in harm's way. These people were not necessarily bad, but they were like many people who tend to act differently when you discuss money with them. Be safe no matter who you are dealing with. Always put everything in writing and have it reviewed by your attorney.

Conduct a Workers' Compensation Audit

Workers' compensation premiums can be one of the biggest costs with regard to your employees. "Workers' comp" is an insurance program that provides insurance to your employees in the case of an accident, injury, or death as a result of being in your employment. The cost of this insurance is paid by the employer and the costs have continued to rise at a very rapid rate. For many companies, this can cost them thousands, even millions, of dollars each year.

The insurance premium charged for this insurance is calculated through a complicated process of examining each employee and assigning them a risk code. It is in making this assignment of risk that many companies are overpaying tremendously. They also frequently miss the opportunity to take allowable deductions and discounts, which costs them even more money than necessary.

The solution is to have your company audited by a company that specializes in workers' compensation insurance audits. Most of these companies will perform the audit free of charge and receive their payment based upon a percentage of the money saved. Statistically, the companies that do this sort of thing say that the average three-year audit produces around $10,000 to $30,000 in a refund to the company that has asked to be audited. One audit that I saw helped a company recoup $130,000 in overpayments. As you can see, a workers' compensation audit could be a big part of finding the money needed to help you eliminate debt. You can contact ForwardFinancialGroup.com for more information about these audits. No matter what company you use, I highly recommend that you have one of these audits conducted. Call 1-800-815-0818 for information about this audit.

Conduct a Telecom, Utility, and Waste Management Audit

If you're like most people, when you receive your phone and utility bills, you assume they are correct and you simply pay them in full. Let me tell you, however, from personal experience that they are not always correct. Several years ago a notation on my phone bill for $50 caught my eye. It seems I was being charged for a Web page that I knew nothing about. This had been going on for seven months without me even noticing it on my bill. After some investigating, I learned that one of my employees had set up a Web page and used the company's phone number on the page. Though I still don't know how it happened, the company that designed the Web page had attached this on-going bill to our company's phone bill.

By some estimates, as many as 90 percent of telecom bills are incorrect. These statistics have been documented from many sources, even the FCC itself. In fact, the FCC stated the following:

> If you haven't completed a detailed analysis of our telecom bill lately there's a 90% chance you are being overcharged—possibly as much as 20%.[1]

> A utility does not automatically give an industrial or commercial customer the best rate when more than one rate is available. It is up to the customer to select the most advantageous rate.
>
> **—The Wall Street Journal**[2]

> 90% percent of all phone bills and 70% percent of all utility bills contain errors. Many of those errors end up costing companies thousands of dollars in overpaid bills.
>
> **—The Northeast Herald**[3]

> Utility bills seem to be getting worse. They are indecipherable, contain inflated or phony charges, and cost customers billions a year.
>
> **—Ralph Nader**[4]

> Over 94% of all bills the phone companies (local and long distance) send out are wrong. As telephone companies introduce more services and the bills get more components and thus more complex, the billing gets worse.
>
> **—Teleconnect Magazine**[5]

These kinds of errors can add up to big money. In 2003 two state employees in Ohio were suspended without pay for allowing two unused phone lines to remain on for six years, which resulted in over payments of $290,000 to the phone company.[6]

This incredibly high rate of error is due largely to a continuing increase in services available and options within each of those services. With consolidated bills such as telecom, utilities, and even waste management, it's not surprising that there is plenty of room for error in the billing process. Like the companies that perform workers' compensation audits, there are also companies that can review your phone, utility, and waste management bills free of charge. They can audit your bills and recover payments going back as far as three years. They also receive their pay based upon a percentage of the money they identify and recover.

Restructure Your Business Debt

If you currently have any kind of business debt, you realize that it is vastly different from home mortgage loans that traditionally offer a fixed rate for up to 30 years. For business (or commercial) debt, most loans are issued for three to five years at a fixed rate. After that, the rate is determined by the prevailing interest rates. This extreme volatility in interest rate charges can put businesses with debt at very high risk. For this reason, businesses must use much caution when considering using debt to keep their operations going.

To stay on top of the true cost of servicing debt, a business owner must be well aware of the upcoming dates for loan renewals, the current rates, and other options available for financing. Many small business owners rely upon their local bank for this service, and in most cases this is a good arrangement. Just like personal debt, part of your financial restructuring process should include looking for ways to reduce the interest that is being paid by your business. In many cases, this debt can be restructured to reduce interest expense and improve cash flow.

Another growing option that is available to small businesses besides their own banks are commercial lending companies. They work with hundreds of lenders and are then able to survey all of them at once and find the best deal for a client. However, before undertaking *any* debt, make a thorough review of your company's current financial standing and debt structure to be sure that any debt restructuring would benefit you. Have your tax accountant give advice on any major changes as well before you act.

When I'm counseling a company about restructuring their cash flow, I always look at the debt structure first. For most of my clients, however, by the time we complete a "looking for money audit," we find enough "extra" money to help them actually eliminate the debt rather than just shuffling it around to another lender. Debt is the enemy of cash flow and in business, cash flow is everything. I always encourage people I work with to stay as "lean and mean" as they can. By that I mean not to expand unless it is absolutely necessary. One rule of thumb I have used is when I feel that I can wait no longer to expand, I wait 90 more days and see if the circumstances are still the same. Sometimes things do change and I'm glad I didn't move too quickly. By using what you have and avoiding debt in your business, you will find that you have more options and more cash flow to use when you are sure.

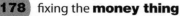

To Lease or Buy, That Is the Question

Deciding whether it is best to lease or buy office equipment can be difficult at times. Over the years, I have both leased and purchased office equipment, and there are advantages and disadvantages to both. When my company's need for copies jumped from the hundreds to the thousands a month, I had need of a more substantial copy machine. When most of our color training manuals began costing us 59 cents a page at the local copy shop, we knew we had to make some other copying arrangements. After researching whether to buy or lease a machine, I opted to purchase a $16,000 copier with cash. That was great for the time being. However, copier technology continued to advance.

Before long, two years to be exact, the newer copiers were able to save me $600 a month by reducing the amount of toner I had been using in the machine I owned. I knew I had to change machines. But this time with my new machine, I decided to lease because I had already been the victim of very fast-changing technology that had made my old machine too expensive to operate. By leasing I could "trade-up" to an improved copier any time throughout my lease. Although it is always cheaper to buy things outright, sometimes other factors need to be taken into consideration. Overall, my belief is that businesses should operate on a cash basis in most cases, but leasing is an option that you may want to weigh out. Leasing equipment does have the advantage of paying just for the depreciated value of the machine while you use it, meaning you are not paying for the residual value that the machine is worth when you are done leasing it. The residual value can work against you however if you are leasing a machine like a copier that has no value when the lease is over. But for a start up business, leasing will work better with your cash flow when you need all of your available cash to operate from.

Leasing allows you to keep your cash on hand to run your business. Leasing is also not recorded as debt. It is basically renting and the payment is a complete write off to the business. However, leasing *is* more expensive than buying, but you have to decide what your money is worth. For instance, if a lease rate is 6 percent and I figure I can invest my money into my business and my business can produce a better return on my investment than 6 percent, then leasing would make sense.

The bottom line is to keep an eye on your overall cash flow needs and not allow your overhead to get very high. The goal is still to be running as lean as you can, while avoiding debt and lease obligations if possible in business. When leasing any item you also want to avoid leasing equipment the first year it comes out. Because the resale value of that item has not had time to prove itself, lenders will keep the residual values low until the resale values prove themselves through time. Remember, leasing does have its place in business and can be an option when looking at cash flow options. Leasing a car, however, is a different story.

Usually I tell people not to lease cars. For example, it usually doesn't make sense to lease a car for business use as most people go over the mileage allowance and it's not cost effective. Most of the time, it makes more sense to purchase a good used car with cash. This allows you to avoid the immediate 20 percent depreciation of buying a brand new car as well as giving you outright ownership of a car with unlimited mileage. The only time I recommend leasing or buying a car on credit is when you have no other options and you have to have a car to go to work and produce income. And if that is the only option someone has, I tell him or her to only borrow enough money for a used car. No new cars allowed. At that point, your motivation is not to own the latest and greatest ride. Instead, you want cheap, reliable transportation that gives you time to save for a better car later, which you will pay cash for.

Employee Benefits and Retirement Plans

There are too many options available concerning employee benefits and retirement plans to go into a lengthy discussion here. I primarily want to make you aware that companies are available to come and review your current plans and present other options that could save you money in these areas.

Frequently, competing companies offer the same benefits plans and retirement packages for a wide range of prices. There are always new strategies to explore as well. In one small company we reviewed, we closed out their 401(k) plan because it brought with it high yearly administrative fees and left the owner with the fiduciary responsibility of the plan's oversight.

The Wall Street Journal reported on Thursday, February 21, 2007, that the Supreme Court unanimously upheld the right of workers to sue their companies over losses in their 401(k) retirement plans if proper communication and oversight of the plan had not taken place. Quoting Gregory Ash, an Overland Park, Kansas pension attorney in the same article: "Employers—or whoever they appoint in their stead—have an established obligation to run retirement plans as "prudent experts" on behalf of participants. Failure to do so can invite litigation."[7]

This employer didn't want to carry that responsibility and risk in such turbulent times. In addition to the risk, his current plan obligated him to a matching contribution for his employees at a 3 percent rate. As cash flow was tightening up, he asked us if there were any options. When we noticed that no one in the company was putting in more than the traditional IRA limit ($5,000 or $6,000 for 2008), we suggested he close out the 401(k) plan and let each employee fund their own IRA account, which we were able to facilitate by bank drafts for them. The employees were now able to custom design their own retirement programs with risk levels they liked, and the employer was now free of all the details of administrating the 401(k) account, free from the 401(k) administration fees, free from being required to fund the 3 percent match, free from the yearly plan filings, and free from the responsibility of the fiduciary oversight of the plan.

As a result, he saved over $100,000 in overhead the first year, which went straight to his bottom line.

After we made these changes and completed our entire audit of his business, the owner then allowed us to complete audits for each of the families in his company. We developed a plan for each employee that helped him or her locate lost money and showed each family how to be out of debt in five to seven years, including their home mortgage. It was like they were given a raise, but their employer didn't have to pay for it. All of the families were excited and the boss was the hero of the company. It was a small project for my company to undertake, but to those who were so positively affected by it, it was an incredibly large project that will benefit them for the rest of their lives.

Conduct a Cost Segregation Engineering Study

What is cost segregation? It's an engineering-based approach to identifying assets within a building that can be reclassified into a much shorter depreciation class than the building itself. Real estate is generally depreciated over time. Commercial property is depreciated usually over 39 years and residential properties 27.5 years. Cost segregation looks at the commercial property with the intent of segregating, or separating for tax purposes, the personal components of the building resulting in accelerated depreciation of certain components of the property. Many parts of the property can now be depreciated at an accelerated 5, 7, or 15-year time frame resulting in thousands of saved tax dollars.

To determine if cost segregation is appropriate for your situation, ask the following questions:

1) Is the cost of your building (not including land) at least $1 million?

2) Have you constructed or renovated any property in the last 12 years?

3) Do you plan on keeping your property over the next few years?

4) Do you have net income that is currently taxed?

Consider the following actual cost segregation engineering report. Suppose a taxpayer purchases a commercial building for $12,135,000, assuming the land is owned by a third party. If the taxpayer does not use cost segregation, he must use the straight line depreciation method of 39 years. In contrast, suppose the owner decides to hire an engineering consultant to prepare a cost segregation study on the property. The engineering consultant shows that of the total purchase price, $11,285,000 should be allocated to the building, $50,000 should be allocated to 15-year depreciation property, and $800,000 should be allocated to a 5-year depreciation schedule. Assuming a 35 percent tax rate, the cost segregation study produces $133,563 in tax savings.

The great news is that there are companies that will do a preliminary study free of charge for your business. The preliminary report will look at your property and tell you how much money a study will save you before you actually initiate a full engineering study.

Check Out Energy Deregulation

With the world demand for oil rising we know that energy prices are going to continue to rise. Energy costs are the third largest expense of U.S. companies, and every company should look at ways to curb energy usage. I know one company that retrained their employees to just turn the lights off when they left a room, and they saved $4,000 a month. One large church that I met with installed a computerized energy monitor, which dropped their electric bill $6,000 a month. Besides watching how we use energy, there are some ways we can actually reduce the cost to purchase it. In many states, deregulation of electricity is allowing consumers to save money. I know of some states where there is a 30 percent difference in energy cost, in the same state, strictly based on the company you choose to buy it from.

Conduct an Energy Audit

There are companies that now do energy audits. They will come into your business and evaluate how you use energy from counting every light bulb to researching how well you are insulated. Most of these companies guarantee a 20 to 30 percent reduction in energy cost to your company in writing. The audits usually have a minimal cost, but there are also implementation costs associated with the changes they suggest you make to your building and energy usage.

Conduct a Property and Casualty Insurance Audit

This audit is a little different than the one I mentioned in the section on buying the right insurance. This one is conducted for businesses by an independent firm that does not sell insurance. Having access to just about every provider and their various rates, this company claims to save businesses about 25 percent on their insurance premiums. The audit is conducted for free but they take a small percentage of the savings they were able to help you find for their time. We found that the savings were worth it.

Use a Credit Card With Bonus Miles to Buy Everything

I use a debit card for most of my expenses in business (U.S. Bank) and I have one credit card also. These cards pay me bonus miles personally for my business expenses. Currently the IRS does not tax redemption of bonus miles unless you convert them to cash. My family has taken many free trips this way. Any business person not taking advantage of the bonus miles on every business transaction is missing out on a good thing. Check with your bank about bonus mile programs. By the way Flexperks offered by U.S. Bank pays triple miles when you use your Visa to donate to a charity!

There's Money in the Small Things

We found that there is money to be found in most everything we do in business. For instance, my company found a payroll processing company that did our payroll at a 25 percent savings over anyone else we found and another company that saved us 30 percent on our Visa card administrative cost. We found a way to save 30 percent on buying bulk office supplies, and we saved 60 percent by switching our phone system to IP Internet lines. We saved travel time and expense by doing most, if not all, of our training through Webinars (GoToMeeting.com), conference calls, and online training modules for our employees.

We also invested money to develop a computer system that enables our clients to input their financial data over the Web. Once our office gets the data, a money coach then calls the client back while at the same time covering solutions for them by a one-on-one Webinar. We save money because now we don't necessarily need to go to our client and incur travel, food, and lodging expenses.

The lesson is that there are a ton of ideas out there that will save your company money. I call these the fragments, and they are worth picking up. Trust me, I have made a life from doing that.

One last thing, back up everything! Did I remind you to back up your hard drive? You can use an online service for this as well as having a separate hard drive in your office. Don't forget to sign up for the free backup for your cell phone contacts also. Most cell phone companies offer this service at no cost but you have to sign up for it. So in conclusion, remember: business is exciting, but making money in business is even more exciting. And money is made (and lost) in the details.

sample business review

summary page showing total savings of
$18,649.33 to the company reviewed

	Service	*Current Spending*	*Final Savings*	*New Monthly Spending*
1.	Corporate Debt Elimination	$23,000	$5,000	$18,000
2.	Electric Deregulation	$2,100	$377.35	$1,722.65
3.	Telecom, Utility & Waste Recovery Audit	$790	$137.73	$652.27
4.	Health Insurance Review	$5,325.63	$1,954.68	$3,370.95
5.	Commercial Loan Review	$5,870.12	$1,327.99	$4,542.13
6.	Investment Review	$4,500	$4,500	$0
7.	Payroll Services Review	$200	$88.04	$111.96
8.	Leasing Review	$3,600	$288	$3,312
9.	Tax Strategies Review	$100	$33	$67
10.	Other Insurances Review	$2,310.88	$562.54	$1,748.34
11.	New Legal Services	$500	$295	$205
12.	Worker's Compensation Review	$625	$235	$390
13.	Cost Segregation	$0	$1,750	-$1,750
14.	R & D Tax Credits	$0	$2,100	-$2,100
	Totals	***$48,921.63***	***$18,649.33***	***$30,272.30***

chapter 15

little-known **hiding places**

In this chapter I'm going to show you some often-overlooked areas for finding money. Some of these may be applicable to you; others won't apply. Of the areas that you do find hidden money, some may provide a major windfall of funds while others offer just a few extra dollars. Whatever the case, the key I want to stress is that it's important to find money wherever you can and watch it add up.

Pay Your Bills Online

This is one of the easiest areas to save money and time. If you pay ten bills online per month, the postage alone would save you $4.10 a month or almost $50 a year. If you figure in trips to the post office, the time and savings really increase.

Take the Mileage Deduction When Volunteering at a Non-profit

As both a businessman and a pastor, I have the privilege of seeing firsthand people volunteer at their church. What most people don't know, however, is that they can claim a deduction for every mile they travel to and from where they are donating their time. If you volunteer twice a week at your church and it is 15 miles from home that's a total of 60 miles per week or 3,120 miles per year. The most recent allowable mileage deduction rate established by the government was 14 cents per mile for non-profit mileage. At this rate, your twice-weekly trips to church would allow you a $436.80 deduction as a charitable donation. If you were to be in the 28 percent tax bracket, that's the equivalent of receiving a check for $122.30 for work that you were going to do anyway. The key to using this option effectively is to keep track of the dates you travel and the mileage.

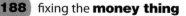

Check for Property Tax Overpayments

This is one area for finding money that I came upon just by accident. Years ago my dad received a notification from his mortgage company telling him that he had overpaid his property taxes three years earlier and that he was due a refund. When I checked it out for him, the mortgage company explained that they had just come across his name on the county's Web site when they were assisting another customer. They were just passing on the news of the overpayment out of goodwill to my dad. When I looked for myself, I found they were completely right—that my dad had overpaid his property taxes, had a refund due him, and that the money was being held by the county should he choose to come and claim it!

As I scrolled through the list of unclaimed money in my father's county I saw there were thousands of families with overpayments totaling over $12 million dollars. In my dad's case, all it took was completing a few government forms and he was sent a check for $3,000 as repayment for his overage. I strongly urge you to check and see if any overpayments are due you on your county's Website.

Review Your Property Tax Assessments

Unknowingly, many, many people overpay their property taxes due to an incorrect assessment of their home's value. *Money* magazine reported in their February 13, 2008, edition that with the decline in home values, 60 percent of the homes in the United States are paying too much property tax. Yet, as little as 2 percent of people go so far as to contest their valuations and simply just pay the amount they are billed. One study indicated that for all challenged assessments, 50 percent result in a positive result for the homeowner. A professional from the accounting firm of Coopers & Lybrand went so far as to say, "Challenging tax assessments is like fighting a traffic ticket—if you show up, you usually get something for it."[1]

The starting place to review your assessment is the local tax assessor's office. Make sure the square footage they are reporting is accurate as well as any changes to your property that might not be reflected in their numbers. After that, compare your home against at least three other homes of comparable size and style in your immediate neighborhood. If your home's value is significantly higher than these, you probably have a case worth challenging. A call to your local assessor will direct you through the next steps. There are also companies that will handle these details for you and charge based upon the money they save you in taxes due.

Check for Unclaimed Money

Not long ago a headline in my local newspaper read, "State Holding $24 Billion Worth of Unclaimed Cash!"[2] As I read further I learned that much of this money comes from abandoned savings accounts, stock dividends, and forgotten paychecks. When unclaimed, businesses are required to turn this money over to the state for safekeeping. One place to start looking is at MissingMoney.com, which is a searchable database sponsored by the National Association of Unclaimed Property Administrators. Not every state is included in this site, so be sure to also check your state's own Web site under the "Unclaimed Funds" link. After I checked the site I found that both of my deceased grandparents had money sitting there to be claimed. You can also check out Unclaimed-Funds.org. Although this site has a fee, it includes over 55 databases including properties as well as unclaimed money. With more then $400 billion in unclaimed funds in the United States, it just may be worth letting your fingers do the walking through a few databases to check and make sure.

Sell Something on eBay

I have learned from watching my father-in-law that what some people consider junk, others are willing to pay a good price for. You just have to know how to find those people, and eBay is an excellent resource for doing so. My father-in-law got his start selling on eBay by posting what I would have considered junk. He simply cleaned out his old shed from out back and before long he had some buyers. It wasn't long after that that my mother-in-law began to miss items from around the house!

It's a pretty safe bet that you'll make more for your unused items through eBay than at a garage sale. Something about pictures posted on the Internet gives items more appeal. eBay is a great place to find that cash you need to develop your cash reserve or to begin your debt elimination plan. Just take a notebook and pen and walk through each room in the house, especially the basement, garage, and closets, and write down everything you do not need any longer or that you are willing to part with. Write these items down and the room you saw them in. Next sit down and begin to formulate what you would take for each item, staying on the conservative side. The next step is to either drop off your stuff at one of the many eBay stores that will sell your item for you for a fee or to go out and buy a digital camera and go into business for yourself. It's like having a treasure hunt in your own house.

Drive One Car

This is a particularly hard option to take for many people looking to find some extra money, but if it is doable in your situation, it can save you a lot. As an example, Allstate insurance says if you only drive your car 10,000 miles a year, it will probably cost you over $6,000 in expenses.[3] Check into carpooling options or having your spouse drop you off at work to free up the car for him or her. Look at this as a temporary fix that is considerably more attractive than a large car payment. All too often I see newlywed couples purchase brand-new cars only to find themselves in deep debt soon thereafter, with car payments too large for their budget. Resist this debt trap and look for ways to save with your cars.

One more bit of advice: if you just can't work this option out, buy some very used cars for cash and drive them as you take control of your finances. The cars may not be your top choice to drive, but as long as they are decent and safe, you can smile driving them knowing that you are saving money each month.

Join the American Automobile Association (AAA).

I highly recommend purchasing AAA's Emergency Road Plan Service. Every year that I have been a member I have saved more through the use of their services than it has cost me. Besides the assistance plan, AAA members also receive discounts at many hotels, trip planning tips, maps, and assistance in planning overseas trips. Through their many services, they can help you with just about any problem you have while being on the road. I put AAA coverage on all the vehicles my children drive as well. It's only one of those small details that help me rest a bit easier when they're out. For more information, go to AAA.com.

Drop Your Credit Life Insurance

When you take out a loan to purchase a car, you are often "strongly encouraged" to buy credit life and/or disability insurance connected to the loan. My advice on both of these options is to say, "No thanks!" Credit life is a very expensive form of life insurance that is paid up-front for the life of the loan. It will pay off the loan if something happens to you. However, the price is usually very high because there is no underwriting associated with it, which means that no medical checkup is required to qualify for the coverage. As a result, healthy people have to pay more than they should to make up for claims by unhealthy people. Besides, the premiums are paid up front and are usually just added to the loan, which means you are paying interest on insurance premiums.

This is also the case for disability insurance that is added on to your loan as it is a single-pay premium too. You can get better rates by owning your own term life insurance and long-term disability policy. These cost less and provide better protection.

If you already have these types of insurance as part of a loan, write a letter requesting the cancellation of the coverage. They will send a refund check to the bank to be applied to your loan balance. Although your payments probably won't change, the length of time to pay off the loan will be considerably reduced.

I also encourage my clients to cancel these types of insurance on any credit cards they have and to make sure their personal term life and long-term disability policies are paid up. Paying off these types of debts in the event of your death is part of what your term life insurance is for.

Sell Your Life Insurance Policy

This is an idea that is growing in popularity as many older people are strapped for cash later on in life. To sell your life insurance policy while you are still alive is called a life settlement. The seller receives a reduced amount of the policy's face value and the purchaser assumes all future premium payments until receiving the full payout at the time of the insured's death. Life settlements are typically aimed at people over the age of 65 with an expected 2 to 15 years of life remaining. Alan Buerger, CEO of Coventry First, a life settlement company, claims that the sale of a policy can "yield four to eight times the current cash value of a policy."[4] The following are actual examples of life settlements:

- A 73-year-old sells a $350,000 policy with a cash value of $15,070 for $60,000;
- A 70-year-old male sells a $175,000 term policy for $84,000;
- A 70-year-old female sells a $750,000 policy with a cash value of $67,000 for $288,000.

Unfortunately, many elderly people don't even realize they can sell their life insurance for cash while they're still alive. Instead they frequently let the policies lapse when the premiums become too much for them to handle financially. Almost every type of insurance policy can be sold including term, whole life, universal life, and variable life. The seller incurs no expenses for the sale as the buyer pays all upfront costs. Although life settlements are generally considered for people over age 65, anyone with a serious illness may qualify. I have even known of older people who have sold more than one policy. They sell their original one and, if their health is still good, purchase another one and then sell it too.

The downside to life settlements is that the insured gives up a large insurance check, which is part of their estate that would have passed to their beneficiaries. Because of this, a life settlement should be thought out carefully. Under the right circumstances selling a life insurance policy can be a financial lifesaver. You can check online for one of the many companies that handle life settlements or go to ForwardFinancialGroup.com for more information.

Drop Your Property Mortgage Insurance (PMI)

Private mortgage insurance is not required by the lender when you owe less than 80 percent of your home's value. This insurance is intended to protect the lender from default and foreclosure losses. The premium for this insurance is priced per thousand dollars borrowed, so on an average home, the monthly PMI premium is $50 to $100. As soon as your loan-to-value falls below 80 percent, it is wise to drop the PMI. Current law states that all qualifying loans that originated after July 29, 1999, give homeowners the right of cancellation when their mortgage balance is less than 80 percent of the original purchase price or the appraised value, whichever is less.

In order to request the cancellation of the PMI, your loan must be current and have had no delinquencies within the last one to two years. In addition, a current appraisal may be necessary and will come at the homeowner's expense. A recent law goes a step further and requires that when a home loan drops below 78 percent of the purchase price, the PMI must be dropped automatically. Unfortunately, this can occur as late as year 13 on a typical 30-year mortgage. If your home has appreciated in value, the loan-to-value ratio may have diminished long before then. If you think you are close to reaching the 80 percent pay-down mark, have an appraisal done and potentially save up to $1,200 a year.

Drop Your Land Line

Because of the widespread use of cell phones by just about everyone these days, it is actually quite easy to cancel your home land line for your telephone and operate solely with cell phones. Many plans also offer free long distance calls, providing another layer of savings over your existing land line.

Just by taking this step, you stand to save $600-$1,000 a year.

Maintain a Good Credit Score

Today your credit score is used for much more than just determining your interest rates on borrowing money. It is frequently used as a benchmark of integrity by potential employers. In my company, we make it a practice to check the credit score of every new applicant before we consider hiring them as a team member.

Knowing this, it is especially important to keep all your payments up to date and your score as high as possible. Because interest rates on retail loans, as well as mortgage rates, are all determined according to your credit score, a low score can literally cost you lots of extra money, which you don't necessarily have to pay. The basic rule is the higher your credit score, the lower the interest rate you will be offered to borrow money. It is up to you to review your credit score periodically to check for errors.

As each of the three big credit scoring services are required to give you one free report a year to help detect fraud, you can request one every four months from first one, then the next, and then the third. Because your credit score is so important in so many areas, the credit rating industry is very helpful when it comes to being aware of your score, maintaining it, and fixing it. Stay away from companies that offer to help clear negative information off of your credit report. If you've been delinquent or defaulted on a loan, work to pay it off, but leave it on your report. To remove it would be lying about your credit history.

Check out the Benefit Bank

The headlines read, "Unclaimed Aid in Ohio: $1.5 Billion a Year." The April 29, 2007 addition of *The Columbus Dispatch*, went on to say, "Low and moderate income families missing out on $1.5 billion a year in government benefits each year turned off by exhaustive paperwork, confusing terminology or long lines."[5]

The Benefit Bank is a free Web-based program that helps people apply for refunds, child care subsidies, rent rebates, medical aid, food stamps, and home energy assistance. It also helps people file tax returns, register to vote, and gain access to many other government programs. The $1.5 billion of unclaimed aid was just for Ohio. Nationally the number is multiplied billions. Those who use the Benefit Bank in the eight states where it now operates found they were able to obtain an average of $6,450 in increased benefits per client. Free software from the Benefit

Bank helps families apply and understand these programs on line. Check it out at TheBenefitBank.com.

Deal With Your Bad Debts

If you have a debt that you were unable to pay at the time it was due, you can usually negotiate with collection agencies to settle for paying 60 to 70 percent of the original amount or less. You must have the cash immediately available as collection agencies will not accept payments over time. Sometimes I find my clients have bad debts from years ago that went into collection and have just never been paid off. Usually the creditor is anxious to get the old loan off of their books and will work with you to reach a settlement amount agreeable to both of you.

Is it ethical to pay less than the original amount of the debt? Not if you are able to pay in full. But it is important to realize that it is the creditor who sets the terms for the settlement, not you. If they are willing to make a settlement with you, they are effectively changing the amount you owe them. If this is agreeable to them, then legally and morally you are released.

Sadly, there are companies that take advantage of these settlement arrangements. They encourage their customers who are looking for a quick way out of debt just to quit paying on their credit cards and to put all the payment money into a bank account. Their strategy is to let the credit card debts go into collections, and then offer the cash they've been putting in the bank as a settlement at a 30 to 40 percent discount. I consider this strategy to be premeditated theft and always caution my clients to steer clear of any outfit offering such advice.

When I present debt settlement, it is for people who find themselves in deep debt but didn't intend to get in so far over their head. As Christians we are to operate in financial integrity. Do remember, though, that if a creditor offers a reduced rate and you accept it with immediate payment, your obligation has been met and your integrity remains in tact.

Research Grants

Most people associate government grants with college expenses, but I have come to realize that grant money is available to just about anyone for just about anything. Currently there are over 20 million people receiving government grants each year. One million of them are entrepreneurs starting or expanding current businesses, 4 million use the money to invest in real estate, 6 million apply the funds to their college education, and the remaining 10 million use the grants to get free training to qualify for a better-paying job.

I saw the benefit of grants firsthand when I recently toured the campus of a local church and was impressed to see that they had just completed a $2 million retirement facility on their property. The pastor told me the entire building was paid for by government grants. There are a lot of books and online resources concerning grants. If you do not have time to research this area, you can hire a grant writer to do this for you also.

Maintain Only One Credit Card

It wasn't long ago that I waited in the grocery store checkout line for the woman in front of me to sort through her 15 MasterCard and Visa cards to decide which one she would use to pay for her groceries. Imagine receiving that many credit card statements in the mail each month!

I am saddened when I see many of my clients try to maintain multiple credit cards. I always advise my families to have only one bank card with a reasonable credit limit. The lower the credit limit, the less trouble you can get into if you happen to go crazy for a time. The credit limit can act as a warning signal that will let you know your spending is getting out of hand and that you need to take steps immediately to correct it. Resist the urge to have individual department stores' branded "revolving charge" cards and the incentive programs they attach to them. Either use one bank-issued Visa credit card or, even better, use a Visa debit card, and you'll be limited by the cash you have available at any time.

Use Jott.com

Jott.com does not really save you money in the truest since of the word, but it can help. Jott.com is a free service that allows you to call a toll-free number from your cell phone and leave a message. Jott then transcribes your message and emails it to your computer free of charge. I have used Jott and it is amazing. When you are driving down the road and you want to remember something, just use your cell phone and when you get home, your message will be in your email inbox. That great idea you get, and can now save, just may be the breakthrough you have been looking for. Try it!

Use Priceline.com

When we travel, we use Priceline for our hotel reservations. Unbelievable savings are available. We always save 50 percent or more. The Website is simple to use for any location and quickly reserves your room at sometimes a 300 percent savings!

Use www.restaurant.com

You can go out for 60 percent less if you buy these discounted gift cards before you go. They have incredible savings and are easy to use.

Use Free Checking

Because most people maintain a checking account, they also incur monthly service fees on these accounts ranging from $5 to $7 typically. If you're still writing "hard copy" checks, look for a bank that offers free checking. Even better, consider using Internet checking because there is no setup or monthly fees and you can pay bills online, transfer money between accounts, and frequently link to other banks. Before you dismiss the charge of only $7 a month for a checking account, take into consideration that if this was invested at 8 percent for 40 years, you would have $24,437 to show for it, instead of just a pile of canceled checks.

Online checking accounts also pay much higher interest then the brick-and-mortar competitors. *Reader's Digest* dated March 2008 states in an article written by Max Alexander, "With no brick and mortar infrastructure to pay for, online-only banks can offer about 5% interest and APY (annual percentage yield) on savings accounts compared with less then 1% at conventional banks." These rates have come down since this article was written but these kinds of differences still exist between brick and mortar banks and online banks. Do some checking and consider doing all your banking on line.

As I said at the beginning of this chapter, some or all of these areas for finding hidden money may be suitable to you. Check into all of them and use all that you can. Every dollar saved is one that you can put toward retiring your debt and getting on the road to living the debt-free life.

chapter 16

everything **family**

In this chapter, I want to focus on areas to save money that center around your family's expenses. Please realize these are just a few of the areas for you to consider. I can speak from personal experience that several of these options have saved my family a significant amount of money and allowed us to reach our goal to get out of debt more quickly and to stay out of debt.

Rethink the Cost of Christian Schooling

In my years of working with families, I have seen many dedicated parents who are clearly committed to giving their children a Christian education, but they go into extreme debt to make it happen. When I review their situations, I frequently end up recommending they consider homeschooling as a way to provide that Christian education at a fraction of the cost.

I remember one family that was facing a tremendous amount of debt and desperately looking for a way to bring their finances into order. They were behind on most of their bills and were facing the possibility of losing one of their cars and maybe even their home. After reviewing their expenses, one single bill stood out among the others. It was their Christian school bill of $700 per month for their three children. This was one of the few bills they were current on. They said it was because they were very committed to educating their children in a godly environment.

When I learned that the mother was a former school teacher, I knew instantly what the solution could be for them, but I decided to wait until I had my facts and figures in order before presenting it to them.

My suggestion for them was to begin homeschooling their children and immediately be free of this large monthly bill to the school. There was no doubt that the mother was very capable, and the couple was clearly willing to sacrifice in order to provide a spiritually grounded education for their children. They were just sacrificing in the wrong area—and sinking their financial future in the process.

When I ran the numbers for them, it was in the context of a plan that showed them being completely out of debt, including their home mortgage, in less than seven years. As I wasn't sure what their reaction would be to my suggestion to homeschooling, I came armed with statistics supporting my idea that proved homeschooling was a viable option they should seriously consider.

I showed them that nationally, homeschooled students tend to perform a grade level above private school students of the same age, and up to four grade levels above their counterparts in public high school. I told them from personal experience that we had homeschooled our five children and that the older ones had easily gone on to college where they maintained 4.0 GPAs. Our oldest daughter even began full-time college at the age of 16 and went on to graduate with honors.

I wanted them to see that homeschooling is a great option for many families. It's growing in popularity across the country, with approximately one million children currently being homeschooled in the country today. Most states have homeschool organizations that can help parents who are new to the concept. These organizations can answer their questions as well as provide a great number of teaching resources. A national organization named Home School Legal Defense Association (HSLDA) even helps to protect and promote homeschooling across the land (HSLDA.org). Many people worry that they can't really teach their children well, but I always tell them to check out all the resources available to them through DVD educational packages and online classes as well as support groups before deciding. There is so much to be gained both academically and socially, and most people are very happy with their experiences. Upon my advice and information, the family chose to homeschool and we were able to put the private tuition of $700 a month back into the budget. This not only dramatically impacted their financial picture but also had a significant impact in a positive way on their children.

Is College Worth It?

An article by the Robertson Education Empowerment Foundation (REEF) makes a strong argument for considering paths other than the traditional four-year college route. In, "The Biggest Gamble of Your Life (Is College Worth It?)," they state that young people ages 18 to 25 gambled away $67 billion in 2005 on college expenses.[1] They took on this expense in anticipation of having a higher earning potential after graduation as opposed to those without degrees. The analysis by REEF comparing college grads against those that went directly into the workforce from high school shows that, in the long run, college may not be the best choice for up to 50 percent of kids.

The study found that with private colleges averaging over $150,000 for a four-year degree, the return on investment is approximately 1.9 percent. For public colleges and universities costing an average of $77,000 for a four-year program, the rate of return on investment jumps to 4 percent. The article also presents the possibility of students taking a job, any job, upon high school graduation and investing the money that would have been spent at a public institution. If invested in a balanced portfolio for the next 40 years, the return would show them considerably ahead financially than college grads were over their working lifetime. The article states:

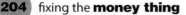

> There are a few important conclusions to draw from these numbers. Conventional wisdom tells parents they should be pushing their kids to college. For many young people this may be awful advice, dooming them to a mountain of debt they will struggle with for decades if not the rest of their life. Exploding costs of higher education tuition (up 35 percent in the last five years and double-digit growth for more than a decade) have far outpaced income growth, making a college education a poor choice for half or more of the population.[2]

Colleges offer academic counseling, but it is up to the student to decide which classes are the most beneficial in terms of impacting their earnings potential. I see families on a regular basis who struggle for years to pay off their old student loans. In many cases, these debts were brought on to complete degree programs that are not even being used in the client's current position. I think it's wise to allow a young person to investigate just exactly what he or she wants to do with his or her life before you invest upward of $100,000 in a college education. Allow young people the opportunity to watch and be involved in an area they are interested in before enrolling in college.

I think many young people would end up in far better shape financially if they or their parents invested in the start-up of their own businesses. Money that would have been spent on college could be put to far better use in giving them a strong start in the exciting and rewarding world of entrepreneurship.

I have faced these questions and concerns with each of my children as they have become older. Drenda and I have taken all these factors into consideration in deciding what is the right path for each of them. As the article concludes:

> There is no data to suggest wages are likely to increase significantly or that college expenses will drop from today's levels, which means we'll see continued deterioration making it a poor choice for even more than half of those attending college.[3]

That's a lot to think about as it concerns your children, and it's a substantial amount of money too.

Look Into Other College Post-Secondary Options

We learned of a great alternative to traditional college when my daughter Amy was only 16 and was ready to begin taking college classes. What we found saved us $28,000 and may be an option for your family as well. This program allowed her to attend college while still in high school. Not only did she receive college credit, but in our particular case, the state paid for the classes.

As I mentioned earlier, my children were homeschooled, and to qualify for the state's post-secondary program, the state required that we legally form our own private school, which amounted to nothing more than filling out a few government forms. As a result, Amy was able to go to college full-time at age 16 for two complete years, which saved us $28,000. Your state may have similar programs that encourage students to begin their college education early and through nontraditional ways. Check your state's education programs and the community colleges in your area.

Another option is to complete classes online or through correspondence. One of the most impressive options in this area is Logos Christian College of Jacksonville, Florida. Their programs offer both hands-on training and class work. In many cases, students are able to receive a B.A. in Leadership and Organization in only two years at a cost of $4,500 a year. That's only $9,000 for a college degree. We felt so strongly about their programs that Drenda and I decided to partner with Logos and now offer the program through our church. For more information, go to Logos.edu.

Determine If Your Teens Really Need to Drive

I stated in an earlier chapter that the average cost to drive a car 10,000 miles a year is approximately $6,000. If the driver is a teenager, that number goes up tremendously. In our family the rule is that our children don't drive until they're 18. We keep this rule enforced for several reasons.

One of the reasons comes from the Allstate Foundation, which says the crash rate per mile driven by 16- to 19-year-olds is four times that of older drivers and that, within that small group, 16-year-olds have insurance rates twice as high as 18- and 19-year-olds. It is statistics such as these that make insurance for teenage drivers so incredibly high. In an effort to encourage safe driving among teenagers, many states also have laws regulating when and under what circumstances young teenagers may drive. Many of these state laws specifically limit the number of passengers to only one other person to limit the number of distractions for a new driver.

By limiting our children's driving privileges until they were 18, we have saved a lot of money. We take the money we've saved by delaying their driving and put it toward helping them purchase their first car when they turn 18.

Don't Go Into Debt to Get Married

With the average price of a wedding fast approaching $30,000, many young couples are getting off on the wrong foot financially and are taking on a large amount of debt just to celebrate their marriage.

Yes, marriage is a covenant that is intended to last a lifetime and should be celebrated and honored, but it's not meant to bring with it the pressure of mountains of unpaid debt after the ceremony. As a parent I see it as my responsibility to counsel my children not to go into debt to get married. I won't have them entering into marriage not understanding the pressures that come with debt.

Those critical days leading up to a wedding ceremony are better spent learning how to succeed in marriage rather than obsessing over the endless details of a "perfect wedding." There are enough challenges when you are first married without adding the stress of unpaid wedding bills to the mix.

I have seen marriages fail because the couple couldn't handle the negative impact such debts caused. In many cases much of the money spent on elaborate ceremonies could be better spent as downpayments on first homes or as an investment in starting a new business.

However the money is allocated, I always counsel young couples just starting out to structure their lives and their finances in such a way that they will have several options available to them when they start having children. Many times I see these young families maxing out their cash flow while the woman is working, and then when the children come they are not financially able to allow her to quit her job. I have faced many new mothers who have pleaded with me in tears to help them find a way to afford staying home with their babies.

I wholeheartedly believe that young couples cannot only win in life financially but also stay out of debt and pay for a house debt free as long as they keep things in the right perspective. To do so, it is important to realize that marriage is a lifetime commitment, not an event.

Decide if Mom Should Work

When many women return to the workplace and place their children in childcare, they fail to realize just how little money they are actually making. In many cases, it's just not worth it for mom to work outside the home.

A recent report on CBS' *The Early Show* broke down the expenses associated with mom's return to the workforce. The report assumed a salary of $40,000. Of this, $15,000 was taken for taxes, $9,600 went to childcare, and $8,160 was associated with miscellaneous expenses such as work clothes and transportation. The result: only $7,180 remained available for other expenses. This broke down to a meager $3.60 an hour![4]

The report went on to explain that through careful management of her family's expenses and activities, it was more beneficial to the family in many areas for mom to remain at home full-time.[5]

Of course, money is not the only consideration when deciding whether it's wise for the mother to work outside the home. Factors such as health insurance, retirement savings, and increased contributions to Social Security for future use should all be considered when making this big decision. Besides the financial advantages, there are also emotional and physical costs that mothers frequently face when returning to jobs, including depression, guilt, and exhaustion. It's a major decision for a family to contemplate and requires research, some financial figurings, and much prayer.

Build Your Own Home

You would be surprised to see how much money you could save by building all or part of your own home. When we built our current home, Drenda and I worked as the general contractors on the construction project and saved thousands of dollars in the process.

After first getting out of debt, we paid cash for our cars and 55 acres of land on which to build our dream home. We were so excited! What we didn't have was the $350,000 it would take to have the home of our dreams built for us. Not long after buying the land, however, Drenda came across an ad for a book titled, *How to Plan, Subcontract, and Build Your Dream House and Save $50,000* by Warren Jaeger.[6]

After reading and re-reading it many times over, we became convinced that we could actually subcontract our own house, even though we had no previous experience building homes. Along the way, we also spoke with many people in the building industry, asked their advice, and realized that this truly was doable for us.

Next we began locating the subcontractors we would need and then began the building process. I remember that on the day we broke ground, it was like a dream. Only a few years earlier we had been completely broke with no future and here we were beginning our dream home on 55 acres of beautiful land that we owned free and clear!

Throughout the building process, we did as much as we were comfortable doing on the construction. I did all the electrical work even though this was my first pass at such a job. I also made sure to have a licensed professional check out all I did to make sure it was safe and up to code. Together we did the tile work, painting, some of the smaller framework and finishing jobs, and the outside landscaping. This was serious work, as in "WORK" with a capital "W," but it was so worth it.

Our original plan was to pay cash for the house as we built it and to take our time while we were living in a rented farmhouse. However, the owner of our rented house sold it, and we suddenly had to be out in three months. We had to abandon our plan to use only cash and went ahead and borrowed enough to finish the house. When the bank came to appraise our finished home, we had $300,000 in equity from day one.

After totaling all our effort that we put into the house, including the general contracting, we estimate that we saved $75,000 to $100,000. Since then I have been a strong voice encouraging others to do whatever they can do when building their own homes. One other book besides the one I mentioned earlier that I also suggest new builders read is *How to Build Your Dream House with No Experience and Save $60,000* by Bryant Clark[7] Looking back, building my dream house has been one of the highlights of my life.

Knowing that it's now paid for and that we helped to build it is a wonderful feeling!

These are just some of the ways we have found money in our family life. Not only have we found extra finances, but extra freedom, peace, and happiness as a result of many of these decisions.

chapter 17

putting it **all together**

I trust the preceding chapters have given you some insight and inspiration about the many ways you can find money in your current circumstances. Of course, there are surely many others areas in which you can find "hidden" money, but these are some of the most productive ones I've found and used.

And finding money is a little addictive. When you find out that you really can get out of debt on your current income, it can spur you to look for other areas to curb spending and accelerate the debt reduction.

The excitement of finding money that is already yours increases with every dollar you uncover. And when you arrive at the wonderful place of freedom from debt, you join the elite minority that no longer lives paycheck to paycheck—one that never worries about being ruined by an unforeseen emergency.

If you've been applying the suggestions and strategies I've laid out in the previous chapters, your efforts are about to pay off. Now comes the fun part! At the end of this chapter, I've supplied a *Summary Sheet* for you to complete (Example 1). There's nothing special about this format. A legal pad works just as well.

First, refer back to Chapter 9 and the forms you completed that identified all your debts and listed your current budget. You'll need the information on those sheets in this chapter to complete your plan. You'll also recall that I gave you an assignment to look for money on your own, anything you saw that could free up money. I mentioned there was the possibility that you could find some cash by selling something or by eliminating a monthly expense like a car payment by selling the car or selling something on eBay. Now get your list labeled *Cash Found* and have your *Summary Sheet* ready to fill in.

You should now have a total of four different sheets of paper in front of you (*Summary Sheet, Cash Found Sheet, Budget Sheet*, and the list of your debts.)

1. On your *Cash Found Sheet*, you should have recorded all one-time-only cash amounts found as you did your assignment in Chapter 9.
2. On your *Summary Sheet* you should record any money you freed up on a monthly basis. If an item is paid yearly, just divide it by 12 before listing it. Again let me say that all items listed here are to be listed on a monthly basis.
3. Now review the last few chapters and identify every money-saving option that you explored and how much money they saved you monthly. If any lump sum cash was freed up in that process, list it on your *Cash Found Sheet* (Example 2). If monthly cash flow was freed up, list it on your *Summary Sheet.*

This process, and some of the items you are exploring, may take some time to actually implement or to research. For now, do the best you can. Use estimates if you are fairly sure that an item applies to you. When finished listing all the cash you've found through your financial restructuring process, add it up. This *Cash Found* list is now going to become the basis of your cash reserve.

Your goal is to start with a $2,000 cash reserve. You should have that amount by now, but if you don't you'll need to take any money that is being freed up monthly and build the cash reserve on a monthly basis until you reach the $2,000 limit before you start any accelerated debt reduction. We will talk more about that later.

For now, just finish the assignment of adding up the amount you now have as your cash reserve. Any money you have above the $2,000 cash reserve goal can be used to pay down debt. For example, if you now have a total cash reserve of $2,400, $2,000 of that would stay in your cash reserve and the other $400 can be applied toward a debt. I always recommend keeping your cash reserve in a different bank than the one where you have your checking account. And under no circumstances do you want to leave your cash reserve in your checking account. It would not last long there. I do not want your cash reserve to be easily accessible. You should really have to make an effort to use it.

Using a money market fund is good, or you could open a savings account, again at a different bank. If you use a different bank, it would also be advised that the bank be a little out of the way. Not one in your office building or your favorite grocery store where you will walk past it each day. An online checking account would also work. Again, I want this money to be a little hard to get to. *It sounds like you don't trust me, Gary,* you may be thinking. Well, you're right. I don't! I'm just trying to help you ensure your success.

Now let's look at that *Summary Sheet*. It should be filled out listing every step that has freed up monthly cash flow over the entire financial restructuring process. List where the money came from and the amount.

You can look at the example at the end of this chapter to get an idea what a *Summary Sheet* looks like when it's completed.

Now here are some additional questions to ask yourself:

Do I Have Extra Money Each Month?

One item that you can now add to your *Summary Sheet* is the amount of money you voluntarily want to apply to your debt elimination plan each month. For instance, maybe you had $500 extra a month before you began my program, and now you realize the wisdom of applying some of this "extra" money toward paying off your debt. For example, if you decide you want to apply $200 each month toward erasing your debt, make an entry on the *Summary Sheet* stating, "Extra Money—$200." If your budget was operating on a negative basis each month before you began my plan, I still want you to enter $100 each month toward debt elimination. It's my belief that just about anyone can come up with an extra $100 a month if they truly believe in the goal they are working toward.

Can I Bring in Extra Work or Overtime During the Process?

Besides looking for hidden money throughout the process, people also are more willing to explore ways they can increase their income, if only for a time. Taking on overtime or a second job are both ways to shorten the length of time it will take you to diminish your debt. God will honor your earnest efforts to be responsible with what He has entrusted to you. I knew of one man who committed to be out of debt within three years. During this time, the man lost his job twice, but God provided new jobs and additional part-time opportunities that allowed him to pay off his debt in just two-and-a-half years instead of three. If you can identify other ways of increasing your income for the short run, add that to your *Summary Sheet* with the notation "Extra Income" and the anticipated amount.

What if I Am Currently Investing in a 401(k) Plan or a Retirement Plan?

Consider a break from investing in your 401(k) plan or company's retirement plan. Such plans are definitely a smart investment in your future. But I often see people putting lots of money into their company's 401(k) plan while living in mountains of debt. My advice is to temporarily stop investing in your 401(k) account until you are out of debt. If you are paying 19 percent on a credit card balance, and only making 8 percent on a retirement plan, it makes more sense to eliminate the higher *negative* percentage rate first.

If you are investing in your retirement account on a monthly basis and you do have a lot of credit card debt at a high interest rate, then make a notation on your *Summary Sheet* that says "Stop 401(k)" and enter the amount that is currently being taken out of your paycheck minus 20 percent to compensate for taxes on this money. You will probably have to notify the employee benefits specialist in your company to stop the deductions. Remember that this is a *temporary* adjustment and that you should undoubtedly reinstate the contributions once you are out of debt.

One exception to this step is if your company is matching more than 50 percent of your contribution. Before stopping the deductions, be sure you figure the total return you are getting with the matching funds. Include your contribution, your employer's contribution, and the rate of return on the total to arrive at this number. If your rate of return is substantially higher than what you are paying in credit card interest, then keep the 401(k) arrangements intact. Most of the time, however, people are so happy to begin paying down their credit card debt that they are willing to forego the retirement contribution for a period. If your contribution to your 401(k) has been sizeable in the past, be sure to check with your accountant about any negative tax consequences that changing your 401(k) contributions might cause since those changes could put you in a higher tax bracket.

Have I Paid Off Any Small Debts With the Extra Cash I Have?

Revisit the *Cash Found Sheet* and determine how much cash remains above your initial $2,000 cash reserve amount. This remaining cash should be used to pay off one or more small debts if possible. Remember that our financial restructuring process has the potential to uncover substantial amounts of money in many areas. Do a thorough review of all these suggested areas to make sure you have explored every available option for finding money.

I generally encourage my clients to apply money found from these areas toward paying off some of your smaller debts first. Even if the interest rates on some of these debts aren't as high as those on some of your credit cards, the emotional satisfaction and personal encouragement you get from eliminating these debts will propel you on down the path to freedom.

If you can now identify any such small debts that can be paid with the cash you have freed up, pay off the smallest one first and list the monthly payment that you were making toward it on your *Summary Sheet*.

From there, apply any remaining funds that cannot completely pay off a small debt to whatever debts carry the highest interest rates. Remember that paying off debt has the same effect as investing. A dollar you keep instead of paying it out as interest has the exact same value as a dollar earned through an investment. Just as you will always want to invest your cash at the highest rate possible, you will also always want to eliminate debts with the highest interest rate in order to benefit the most.

How Much Am I Saving Monthly?

Return to your *Summary Sheet* when you feel confident that you have listed every bit of money that you have freed up on a monthly basis. Then add up the monthly savings column on the right. This number is the total amount of money that you now have made available on a monthly basis through your financial restructuring review.

From here we can begin accelerating the debt elimination portion of the plan. The key to accelerating your debt elimination is to maintain your total current monthly cash flow toward all your debts. In other words, when a debt is paid off, its normal payment does not go back into the budget as free money; it's now rolled into the current payment of another debt. Continue applying monies freed up from individual debt payoffs toward the next debt until all your consumer debt is gone.

Across 27 years of helping others in this way, it has been my experience that most people can pay off all of their consumer debt, as well as their mortgage, within five to seven years with this method. Amazingly, this can frequently be accomplished without an increase in income. Not always, but in over 70 percent of the families I've assisted that have followed the program, this has been possible.

How Fast Will I Get out of Debt?

My company has a program that can accurately calculate how soon you will be debt free based upon your specific numbers. You can enter your data and receive a free printout by going to FaithLifeNow.com and clicking the financial life button. However, you can do these calculations yourself with a few formulas.

First, add up all the debt you have remaining at this point. Get the average interest rate of these combined debts or make an educated guess as to the average. Keep in mind that the larger debts like your mortgage will pull the average down.

Using a financial calculator, solve for N using your total debt amount (PV), the total amount of money you have available to pay toward debt each month (PYMT). This would include the money that you freed up plus the amount of the normal scheduled payments. And finally you will need to enter your average interest rate that you are using (INT). When you solve for N you will get the total number of months it will take to pay off all of your debt. You will need to divide this by 12 to find the number of years required.

Hold on and prepare to be encouraged. I think you will be very surprised at just how fast you can get out of debt.

Am I Committed to Implementing the Plan?

Our plan is a road map to freedom. It's not that the plan has any special ability to set you free, but through its implementation you will soon begin to experience glimpses of financial freedom. Be patient as you work through each of the chapters and the assignments. The implementation can take time to do thoroughly and usually involves working with several outside companies and professionals that specialize in some of these areas.

I want to remind you that I have counseled you throughout this process to keep your cash reserve separate and apart from your other financial accounts. The goal is to help you administrate this plan to keep it safe from its most dangerous enemy—you. Yes, the person most likely to derail your progress toward freedom is the one looking back at you in your mirror! I want you to take steps to make deposits into your reserve automatic so that you remove the temptation to dip into the "extra" money for something you might regret later.

The first step is to establish what I call your G.O.D. account. The letters G.O.D. stand for your "Get Out of Debt." This G.O.D. account represents a checking account that will pay the acceleration portion of your debt payments from now on.

Don't allow the freed-up money to go into your regular checking account at all. Rather, have it deposited into your G.O.D. account. Just like your cash reserve account, we want to keep this money separate.

Let me state this another way: Previous to undertaking our debt restructuring program, you were spending a set amount of money on your debts and living expenses. When you adjusted some of your expenses through your search for hidden money, you freed up what is hopefully a significant amount of cash flow. In other words, you now have money available to you that previously wasn't there.

Understanding human nature, there will come sooner or later a time when you will be tempted to spend some or all of this "new" money. Even people with the best of intentions give in and dip into this money. They don't plan to, but it just happens somehow. To prevent this from even being a temptation, I want you to put all the "new" money into its own account, clear and separate from all other monies. This account doesn't necessarily need to have unlimited checking as you will probably only be writing one or two checks on the account each month.

To use the G.O.D. account, divide the total monthly amount of money freed up by the number of your pay cycles in a normal month. For example, if you identified $1,200 a month in your restructuring process and you are paid weekly, you would break that $1,200 down into 52 pay periods, which equals $276.92 a week. Now this $276.92 needs to come out of your regular checking account each week as soon as you are paid. When you get your regular weekly paycheck, *immediately* write out a check and deposit slip to your G.O.D. account. I strongly urge you to mail it right away so that you don't find yourself out shopping and realize the extra money is there and available to spend.

At the end of each month, empty your G.O.D. account and apply it to the debt you are working on for that month.

Remember, we are going to accelerate the payoff of one debt at a time. When the debt payment that you are working on at the time comes due, write your normal payment from your regular checking account and then write a second check from your G.O.D. account for as much as has been put in there this month. Your payment should have two checks with the invoice—one from your regular account and one from your G.O.D. account with the acceleration amount written on it. As each debt is paid off, add its usual payment (which is now available since it is paid in full) to your G.O.D. account weekly deposit. This way, as long as you make your G.O.D. account deposits each pay cycle, you can spend the rest of your money with freedom knowing that you are on track to be debt free in the time period you have planned for.

What Debt Should I Pay Off First?

As I explained earlier in the chapter, I normally recommend paying off the smallest debts first to begin freeing up cash immediately and to generate excitement and momentum. There is, however, one debt that I advise making a priority for payment above all others—any debts to family members.

When you owe a relative—whether or not they have charged you interest—your relationship is almost always affected in some way. For the peace of mind of having that debt clear and to maintain your integrity within your family, I almost always recommend paying family first.

This is especially important to your Christian walk, as family members who are not believers will see you demonstrate godly character by being responsible for your debts.

One other possible exception is the possibility of paying off a loan with a low interest rate *if* by paying it off you will free up a significant amount of cash. An example would be to finish paying off an account if only a few payments remained and then this debt would be completely erased. Occasionally, by paying off some of these smaller debts quickly from the start, a wife is able to stay home with the children and invest further in their education and growth.

What About Emergencies?

Write it down and plan on it—something *will* break and need to be replaced before you get to the point where you are completely debt free. Your cash reserve should be your first means of meeting the expense. If this is not enough, consider other alternatives for getting the funds and factor in their impact on your debt elimination plan.

For example, if your car needs to be replaced, that would probably mean going into debt to get another one. Until you are able to purchase the car you really want, buy a very used vehicle to meet your minimum needs. This will allow you to keep your new debt to a minimum. For whatever the emergency, if you empty your cash reserve account, redirect the deposits from your G.O.D. account to your cash reserve account temporarily. Once you again have a balance of $2,000, then switch the deposits back to how they were originally.

Though I don't especially like the idea of taking on new debt in the middle of a rigorous debt elimination plan, sometimes circumstances make it unavoidable. Finding yourself without transportation can be such an occasion. For most of the other emergencies, you will probably be able to handle them with money from the cash reserve account. Remember to replace the money spent for the emergency in the cash reserve account as soon as possible before you return to funding your G.O.D. account. Sometimes these emergencies can extend the completion of your plan by a few months, but most families are so intent on completing the program, they stick with it diligently in spite of having an emergency.

If you are like most people, when you see how quickly you can be debt free you will find it hard to believe. You can do this! It will take a little time to set up, but it is so exciting to see your freedom become a reality. My advice to you is simple—go for it!

summary sheet

	Source of Monthly Cash Flow	*Amount Freed Up Monthly*
1.		$
2.		$
3.		$
4.		$
5.		$
6.		$
7.		$
8.		$
9.		$
10.		$
11.		$
12.		$
13.		$
14.		$
15.		$
16.		$
17.		$
18.		$
	Total Monthly Freed Up Cash:	$

CASH FOUND

Source of Money Found	Amount Found
1. CASH ON HAND	$ 300
2. GARAGE SALES	$ 737
3. EBAY	$ 300
4. SOLD OLD BIKES	$ 100
5. SOLD SCOOTER	$ 350
6. SOLD OLD FURNITURE	$ 250
7. RECEIVED GIFT	$ 100
8. TAX REFUND	$ 3,000
9. SOLD COMPUTER	$ 100
10. TOOK OLD CHINA TO AUCTION	$ 250
11.	$
12.	$
13.	$
14.	$
15.	$
16.	$
17.	$
18.	$
19.	$
TOTAL	$ 5,487

Summary Sheet

(Example One)

Source of Monthly Cash Flow	Amount Freed up Monthly
1. REFINANCE	$ 230
2. CONSOLIDATE LOANS	$ 476
3. PAID off CAR	$ 366
4. STOPPED CABLE TV	$ 55
5. INSURANCE REVIEW	$ 98
6. REMOVED PMI	$ 85
7. DROPPED MEMBERSHIP	$ 65
8. CHANGED TAX WITHHOLDING	$ 285
9. STOPPED 401K	$ 135
10. CHANGED CELL PHONE PLAN	$ 15
11. PD off MEDICAL Bill	$ 65
12. SOLD MOTORCYCLE	$ 166
13. CHANGED HEALTH INS	$ 85
14. PAY bills ONLINE	$ 4.50
15. TAX PLANNING	$ 230
16.	$
17.	$
18.	$
Total Monthly Freed Up Money	$ 2,360.50

chapter 18

investing in your future

If you have followed the strategies and steps outlined on the preceding pages, then you are well on your way to financial freedom. So what do you do once you get there?

I believe we find an answer to that question in Genesis 41:33. There, God gave Joseph a plan that would save the entire nation of Egypt, as well as his own family, from certain death. That same plan is available to you today and still has the power to save you and those you love from a future of slavery—slavery to debt.

Joseph was the youngest of 12 brothers and, because he was his father's favorite, his brothers despised him. You know the story. One day, in their jealousy, they sold Joseph into slavery and reported to their father that he had been killed by a wild animal. The traders took him to Egypt where they sold him to a man named Potiphar, a captain in the Egyptian army. Unfortunately, during this time Potiphar's wife made continual advances toward Joseph, but he refused every time. Angered by the rejection, she told her husband that Joseph had attacked her and he was then thrown in jail.

It was there that Joseph developed a reputation for being able to accurately interpret dreams. When Pharaoh himself had a dream that he could not understand, an ex-prisoner mentioned Joseph to him. Pharaoh called for Joseph and told him this dream:

He saw himself standing by the Nile, when out of the river there came seven cows, sleek and fat, and they grazed among the reeds. After them, seven other cows, ugly and gaunt, came up out of the Nile and stood beside those on the riverbank. And the cows that were ugly and gaunt ate up the seven sleek, fat cows.

Joseph told Pharaoh that the seven good cows meant seven years, and the seven ugly cows were seven years also. The seven ugly cows represented seven years of famine and the seven fat cows represented seven years of abundance. Joseph went on to explain to Pharaoh that the next seven years in Egypt would be years of great abundance, but the following seven years would bring a famine so severe that the seven years of abundance would be forgotten.

Joseph then told Pharaoh that he should appoint a man who could organize a plan to save a fifth of Egypt's crops over the next seven years, which would be available during the time of famine. Pharaoh was so impressed with Joseph that he put him in charge of this plan and Egypt was saved. Joseph's own family was also saved when they came to get grain from Egypt. The plan that saved Egypt was a simple one that we need to follow today as well.

The plan was simply this: do not spend everything you make today, but remember to put some back for the future.

I have already written a lot about the importance of a cash reserve and its ability to provide a "cushion" when you experience one of life's sudden expenses. The same thing is true of your retirement accounts. They protect your future ability to live in financial freedom even after your earning years are winding down. Your retirement accounts also cushion you from the ravages of inflation that are sure to eat away at every dollar you've earned. Here's a picture from my personal experience of what inflation can do to your wealth.

In 1997, I bought my current homestead land of 55 acres for $88,000. Today, that same land is worth $300,000. If I think even further back, all the way to 1974, my sister's then-new Camaro cost a whopping $4,000. Today, that car would cost $40,000! What you consider to be an adequate income today will probably land you on the streets 30 years from now. You don't need a dream to tell you to plan for the days ahead and to start saving now.

Fortunately, you are already on the right path to enjoying a prosperous future. You're getting out of debt as quickly as possible. Following Joseph's wise counsel to the Pharaoh, we need to use our current earning years to prepare for the possible lean years ahead. Just by having your home mortgage paid off and being completely out of debt, you will be light-years ahead of so many Americans who will be struggling to simply get by in the years to come.

As you move from being a slave to debt to being free from debt, you will need to find viable options for investing your future nest egg. There are tons of investment options available these days. Some are a lot riskier than others. It's important to keep in mind that there is some element of risk in just about any investment vehicle.

I have been involved in helping people invest for their futures for 28 years now, and for most of that time I recommended mutual funds as the vehicle of choice for long-term investing. But something happened in March 2001 that affected how I thought about investing and I altered my advice.

In March 2001, the markets began a three-year slide that took $8 trillion dollars of equity out of the markets. The terrorist attacks of September 11, 2001, helped plunge the stock market into a freefall that hasn't been seen since the Great Depression. During this market decline, 52.7 million households saw their retirement accounts drop 50 to 70 percent. Many people who were anticipating retirement in the near future were forced to delay that decision to compensate for their losses. Others lost everything they had ever worked for.

In my study of world events, politics, and the U.S. economy, I realized that this type of market swing could happen again, and it did in 2008. Because I bring a conservative nature both to my personal life and my business, this was clearly something I took into serious consideration when counseling my clients about their financial futures. As a result, I no longer felt comfortable recommending mutual funds to my customers as the primary investment tool for long-term investing. I had been on both ends of the investing spectrum and had come to appreciate conservative options.

When I had no money and was in debt, I searched for aggressive opportunities that could bring big, fast returns on my money and help me make up for "lost" time being in debt. When I got out of debt and had large sums of money that I had worked long and hard to save, I still wanted a vehicle with strong growth potential but with little risk. I had worked too hard to gather that money and couldn't bear the thought of it simply vanishing in a stock market downturn. These were the goals that prompted me to set up my own company to offer conservative advice when it came to long-term investing.

Even back when I had used mutual funds as my primary investment vehicle for years, I did so with a conservative, skeptical mindset. I searched out the conservative funds that had long track records of performance data that gave me insight concerning how well they did in a bear market, not just how they performed in a rising market. (Almost everything does well when the markets are rising.) But suddenly, even the conservative mutual funds I leaned to for years seemed to be too exposed for my comfort. So I began a search for conservative products that could provide growth potential and at the same time protect my clients' principal from sudden market swings.

What I found shocked and excited me. I was dumbfounded that I had not been made aware of this new investment vehicle even though, at the time, it had been out for several years.

I'm referring to a totally new concept called an **Equity Indexed Annuity (EIA)** that had its debut in 1995. I suppose the reason I'd never taken the time to investigate this option was because the word *annuity* threw me. Typically over the years I had not recommended annuities to my clients because of the low rate of return they paid out. When variable annuities were introduced to the market, I turned my clients away from them due to their high fees and management expenses, which reduced their net return by 1 percent to 3 percent.

"Just buy the mutual fund yourself and put it in an IRA and you will do better," is what I told my clients. So when I heard the word annuity I didn't get too excited. It was only after the three-year free fall of the markets that I was now willing to search through options that I had not explored before. When I finally looked at the equity index annuity products, I couldn't believe it. They seemed too good to be true. I reviewed the data again and again.

I finally made the decision that from this point on, my company would stop recommending mutual funds and start recommending EIAs as the preferred investment vehicle for my client's safe money. I define safe money as money that my client is unwilling to lose. I knew this decision would be challenged by some, but I remained confident that for my clients and my conservative investing nature this would be the product I would endorse. Since that day, my firm has moved millions of dollars into EIAs and I've never looked back.

Let me give you a brief overview of how EIAs work.

Imagine a product that allows investors to participate in the market's upward movement but not in the downward movement. Any yearly gains made by the EIA are locked in. Once index-linked interest is credited to an index annuity, it cannot be lost, even if the market index declines after that. Money that you make over the course of the year becomes part of your guaranteed principal forever. On the other hand, with mutual funds you can have a great year but see your gains wiped out the next year if the market is in decline. The gains in an EIA are tied to a market index such as the Standard & Poor 500, NASDAQ, Dow Jones, and the RUSSELL 2000. In review, you get market type performance but with no downward market risk—none! Once an annual gain is realized it becomes part of your principal forever!

With an EIA, an insurance company uses your premium (your investment) to buy bonds that will equal the principal you have deposited in the EIA upon maturity. The insurance company then buys stock options on the stocks that make up the index you have selected.

One important point to remember here: stock options are not the same as being invested *in* the market. An option gives the holder just that—an option, to buy or not buy a particular stock on a future date after the performance of the stock is known. In this way, EIAs can capture some, not all, of a market's upward activity without putting your money in the markets directly.

In his book *Index Annuities*, Jack Marrion explains that the reason you don't realize all of the gain is because it costs the insurance company something to provide against the possibility of a loss.[1]

So while you don't fully participate in the gains if the market goes up, you also won't lose principal in a falling market. Thomas Brueckner of Senior Financial Resources, Inc. estimates that typical EIA investors will participate in 55 to 80% of the market's performance.[2] For example, let's say during a given point in time the S&P 500 was averaging 10.11 percent over 12 months. If you owned one popular EIA that I recommend, you would have received 8.71 percent return after expenses.

You might question whether an 8.71 percent gain instead of a 10.11 percent return is worth the protection. To answer that question, you need to realize that most mutual funds do not deliver the full performance of the market either. They can't.

In his *Wall Street Journal* article, "The Emperor's New Mutual Funds," writer John Bogle plays on the popular children's story *The Emperor's New Clothes*, in which the emperor seemed to be above the facts, including the fact that he had no clothes on. In the story, no one was brave enough to tell him the truth. And so, as long as no one told him differently, he never realized how truly wrong things were. Bogle likens investors to the uninformed emperor because they are operating without knowledge of how things really are. "Investors seem largely unaware of the substantial gap by which stock, bond, and money market funds lag the returns of the markets in which they invest," says Bogle, "While the S&P 500 Stock Index has risen at a 12.2% average annual rate since 1984…the average equity fund has grown at a 9.3% rate."[3]

Obviously that quote was taken from Bogle before things went downhill in the markets because the actual return in the S&P over the ten years prior to March 2010 has been –.64 percent. However his assessment of the EIA concept is still valid. He continues with his explanation of the differences in return due to the high costs incurred by mutual funds.

> The costs of playing the game are surprisingly large. They include mutual fund expense ratios, which reached an all-time high of 1.6% of equity-fund assets last year. Turnover costs, by conservative estimates, total another eight-tenths of 1%. Adding the impact of sales charges, out-of-pocket fees, and other expenses, "all-in" costs for the average equity fund come to as much as 3% per year.[4]

So as you can see, our 8.71% yield in our EIA is not really too far removed from the true average returns.

With this kind of performance as the norm, EIAs offer a compelling choice, especially when you factor in that they bring with them no exposure in a downward market. Apparently my company is not the only one that has been promoting EIAs as they have grown in popularity at a very rapid rate over the past few years.

Besides their increasing popularity, many EIAs also offer an initial bonus on new money invested in an account. One EIA in particular offers an 11 percent bonus on new money going into the account and continues to offer the bonus for any future new money invested in the account for seven years. This means that on the day you open your account, the insurance company immediately credits your account with 11 percent of your initial deposit. That bonus money is yours to keep and it participates in any future gains that your EIA produces from that point forward.

EIAs also have many liquidity features that give them flexibility in meeting the cash flow needs of their investors. Typically, 10 percent of the current account value can be withdrawn each year without penalty. There are many monthly income options that can be started and stopped throughout the life of the annuity without giving up the availability of the principal balance. I consider the only possible drawback to EIAs to be their early withdrawal penalty. Because the collateral behind the accounts are bonds, EIAs are designed to stay in place for a number of years. If the product is cancelled before the bonds mature, the company incurs fees and costs that will be passed on to you, the investor. Because of this, EIAs are not suitable for everyone, but they fit well with most retirement objectives. From my experience, the many liquidity options they offer more than offset the downside of the early withdrawal penalties in the standard EIA.

Most EIAs offer a 2 to 3 percent interest rate guarantee on deposited money. This interest rate guarantee is a safety net of sorts. This means that even if the markets go down every single year you are invested in the product and you have no credited gains from market performance, you would still be guaranteed to get your principal back plus the interest. Mutual funds can in no way make that offer. I have clients from all walks of life who have invested in EIAs. My firm currently invests millions of dollars into them every year.

EIAs come in all kinds of maturity options to give customers a range of choices in planning for their future. You can find EIAs with maturity periods as low as four years and up to 14 years. EIAs typically have no administration fees, annual fees, or broker fees involved so every penny you invest goes into your account. EIAs also qualify to be used as IRAs, 403(b)s, and most other qualified retirement plans.

I'm frequently asked if an EIA can be used in a 401(k) at work. Currently, I don't know of any EIAs that are available to be used within 401(k) plans. However, a law passed in 2002 made it possible to move your current 401(k) vested money into a qualified IRA that can then be put into an EIA while you maintain your 401(k) and without you having to quit your job to get it. This rollover can occur with absolutely no tax consequences to the investor. We have moved many 401(k) monies into EIAs. It's important to check the specifics of your 401(k) program because, although the law was enacted, each 401(k) must amend their respective plan documents to allow the change. To find out if you can move your 401(k) plan, ask your current plan administrator if you can take a non-hardship in-service withdrawal without suspension into a qualified IRA account. If your plan allows for it, your employer should also be able to tell you how much qualifies for the transfer.

I firmly believe in the EIA concept and recommend that you check out the options for yourself. For my clients that come to me with mutual fund-oriented investments and IRAs, I tell them to move them to EIAs.

Of course, you need to evaluate the circumstances of your particular financial situation and seek competent advice before altering any accounts—investment, retirement, or otherwise. You can contact my firm Forward Financial Group at 1-800-815-0818 for more information about EIAs nationwide. We would be glad to help determine if they are right for you.

Regardless of where you put your money, you need to remember the importance of putting some away for the future. If you don't opt for EIAs, take advantage of the many **qualified IRA plans** available. By using traditional IRAs, Roth IRAs, 403(b)s, 401(k)s, and SEP IRAs, you can maximize your nest egg's potential.

After you get out of debt, the money you were previously using to service the debt is now available to invest. I suspect you'll be surprised at how fast you can accumulate a large amount of cash. When we first got out of debt and began saving, it wasn't too long before we had saved $100,000. People asked us all the time how we did it. I told them what had worked for us by asking them a question: "If you had no debt payments of any kind, how much money would you be able to save every month?" They soon got my point and realized that debt was holding them back from saving tremendous amounts of money. As a result of my simple question, I have seen families be able to save hundreds of thousands of dollars once they got out of debt.

In closing, I want to share a warning. It's probably not necessary. You have probably already absorbed this wisdom from the previous comments, but I want to be sure you're straight in understanding my advice.

I've met many people through the years who, in hopes of making big gains quickly, try to invest directly in the stock market. Some try to play commodities futures or options. Others think day trading is their ticket to fast riches.

Even a former employee of mine fancied himself a day trading whiz for a while. He thought he had found a formula, and it seemed to work for him for a while. He made a little bit of money at it early on and began telling his family and friends what he was doing. "Easy money," he called it. So his family members started giving him *their* money to invest for them. Not too long after that something affected the market negatively and his "sure thing" formula failed him. He lost $20,000 of his brother's money.

Sadly, I've seen this (and similar things) happen time after time. I strongly caution you not to do it.

Lastly, I want you to be especially wary of the allure of **money schemes, the lottery, and multi-level marketing** (MLM) businesses.

I had one friend who became involved in a network marketing "opportunity." Although he was excited about it, every time he told me about it, something just didn't sound right. Sure enough, the "opportunity" ended up costing him $20,000 and quite a few friendships.

Watch out for the latest MLM as they are always coming and going. Having worked with thousands of people and served as a pastor, I've seen dozens of MLMs work their way through a community of people, only to fizzle and leave many people without their initial investment. People usually get excited about MLMs in the beginning, buy $5,000 worth of products, and have little to show for their investment a few months later. I have had to help hundreds of families work to pay off Visa card debt that was piled up by buying into an MLM and the associated upfront costs.

I'm not against MLMs per se. Just those that tend to prey on people's desire to get rich quick—which, as it turns out, is the majority of them.

Some of my best friends make hundreds of thousands of dollars a year from MLMs. My rule of thumb is to judge the MLM by the product and the cost of the product. If the MLM is system-motivated, meaning they are more concerned about the grids of different selling levels than they are about the product, don't even consider becoming a part of them. If, on the other hand, you and the company fully believe in the product, and the product is priced appropriately and meets people's needs, then consider it as a worthwhile investment of both your time and money. Just know from the start that you will not find an instant ticket to financial freedom no matter what the slick marketing pieces claim.

No matter how you go about getting out of debt, you have to know from the start that it will take diligence and integrity on your part to make it work. Just like my life was changed dramatically the day Drenda and I committed to trusting the Kingdom of God, yours will be too when you make that major decision. Trust in the Lord to lead you in wisdom and choices. Take it one day at a time and success will be yours.

chapter 19

finding your **purpose**

In virtually every chapter of this book I've either shared serious reasons for getting out of debt or powerful ways to do it. Because of that, you might be tempted to assume that helping you achieve that freedom was the highest purpose of this book. But you'd be wrong.

For all I've taught, explained, recommended, and counseled about getting out of debt, it's important that you know financial freedom is not the end of your journey. No, it should be the beginning.

As I've learned since first becoming debt free, it is only when you can win at the money game that you can truly find out what life is all about. Since the early days of my business, I have told my clients that until they fixed the "money thing," they could never find their destiny. You may consider this a harsh statement and even doubt its validity, but the bottom line is that I didn't say it, Jesus did. In Matthew 6:24, Jesus was teaching about the Kingdom of God when He said:

> *No one can serve two masters. Either he will hate the one and love the other, or he will be devoted to the one and despise the other. You cannot serve both God and Money.*

Jesus is unequivocally saying that there are two systems in life, two kingdoms, and you can't serve both at the same time. You'll serve the master whom you most trust to meet your needs. It doesn't matter how much you jump and shout in church, when you've got to make a significant life decision, you'll always default to the one master you consider most capable of meeting your needs. Let's review where things went wrong.

> *"...Cursed is the ground because of you; through painful toil you will eat of it all the days of your life. It will produce thorns and thistles for you, and you will eat the plants of the field. By the sweat of your brow you will eat your food until you return to the ground..."* (Genesis 3:17-19).

Remember, when Adam rebelled he forfeited God's ability to provide for him. Adam instantly became a survivalist. From that moment on, his entire life became consumed with the quest for provision. Every thought he had would be filtered through the finding-provision mindset.

He was no longer free. He became a slave to the earth-curse system of lack and poverty. The only way out of this system was to sweat with painful toil all the days of his life. Humankind has lived under that weight of slavery from then until now.

As I stated back in Chapter 7, this is why the lottery is so appealing. It seems to offer us a chance to finally get out from under the constant weight of looking for provision. We are tired and we all want to stop running. Everyone wants to become a millionaire because that is the only ticket out of the rat race. We're tired and want to find rest from this system of fear and worry and lack.

Now let me take this a step further. When Adam lost his provision, it was not the only thing he lost. You see, when Adam lost his provision, he lost his vision for his life. His vision became one of just surviving each day—running after money, or hoarding money if he had it.

Take a look at the word *provision.* I say it this way: provision is pro-vision. To put it in other words, if you have no provision, what vision you do have will die.

For example, if a man's wife says she needs a bigger house and he has no money, he cannot pursue that vision. That vision will die.

So when Adam lost his provision, he lost his vision. He also lost his assignment. Remember, Adam was not placed on the earth just to sit around. He was told to tend to God's Garden, or we could say he was to be about Father's business. When Adam lost his provision he had to let go of his assignment, his created purpose. His whole life was now dedicated to finding provision .It became his vision and his assignment. But in that process he had to abandon his spiritual DNA, his reason for creation and living. That's why Jesus tells us that man cannot serve two masters. It is simply not possible. Jesus then goes on to explain this further in Matthew 6:25:

> *Therefore I tell you, do not worry about your life, what you will eat or drink; or about your body, what you will wear. Is not life more important than food, and the body more important than clothes?*

In this verse, it's clear that Jesus already knows how most of us live—in a constant state of worry. Worry about provision. Worry about what you need. Worry about how you're going to get it. Worry. Worry. And then some more worry. But what is Jesus' response to all this fear and anxiety?

He says, "There is no need to worry. There's another system, another Kingdom that has abundant provision in it." When you learn how to tap into it, you will find the things you have need of in life. He tells us that the things of life were created to serve us, not the other way around. When we run, run, run to pay for everything we need and want, we're being a servant to the thing rather than the thing serving us. Think it through, and you'll quickly realize that homes, cars, clothes, and *anything* else you can name were created *for* you to use, not for them to *use* you.

Most people, whether they are Christians or not, have it all backward and spend their days running and running, oftentimes to the point of exhaustion. The reason that Christians are no different from nonbelievers in this instance is because they are trying to find their provision the same way unbelievers are—you guessed it, by running. Most believers have not been taught how to tap into the Kingdom of God and how to free themselves from the earth-cursed system of slavery to debt.

A Pastor Finds That the Kingdom of God Works

I first met Pastor Brown when he attended an inner-city pastors' meeting I was conducting. I was teaching on the Kingdom of God and how it operates. When the meeting was over, Pastor Brown and his wife approached me. I could tell just by looking at them that they were troubled about something. They looked worried.

He told me that they wanted to give to the ministry and asked us to pray for them as tears welled up in his eyes. Drenda and I laid our hands upon him and prayed. That was the end of our first meeting.

Three months later I was teaching at an inner-city church and looked up to see Pastor Brown. He asked if I remembered him and I assured him that I did. He then proceeded to tell me how moved he and his wife were when they heard my teachings about the Kingdom of God and how it works. He said that when they left my meeting, they both felt the need to release their desperate financial situation into the Kingdom of God. He went on to explain that despite the fact that they were in danger of losing their home in five days if they didn't come up with $6,500, they gave their last $100 to the ministry that evening.

Almost immediately after releasing their future to God's Kingdom principles, the small screen printing business they had been running to supplement their ministry income suddenly took off. In the five days after they released their last bit of money into the Kingdom, the business brought in $8,500, more than they had ever made in a full month before. "I just want you to know that the Kingdom of God works," he said, smiling as he walked away.

I smiled too, but that was because I was thinking to myself that nothing really unusual had happened. Pastor Brown had just tapped in to the Kingdom of God. It's the same Kingdom that is available to you too.

In that same passage in Matthew, Jesus gives us some great insight into why His Kingdom works in this way:

> *Look at the birds of the air; they do not sow or reap or store away in barns, and yet your heavenly Father feeds them. Are you not much more valuable than they?* (Matthew 6:26).

In this verse, Jesus takes one of the simplest, commonest creatures on earth—birds—and points to them as our example.

They don't depend on their ability to sweat with painful toil for everything they have. You won't find birds working at their extensive worm farms, stockpiling worms for the future. They don't lose sleep because of worry or make themselves sick with stress.

They do, however, gather what they need from what God has provided for them. Jesus was telling us to learn from the birds. He wants us to know that in the Kingdom of God, we don't need to worry and take upon ourselves the weight of sweating by painful toil for everything we will ever have need of over the course of our entire lives. Talk about relief! God takes care of the birds; they just simply gather what God has already placed there for them when they need it. We are to gather in the same way as we stay with our created purpose and assignment.

Remember back to my discussion of this in Chapter 7? When Peter had taxes to pay, Jesus didn't tell him to go get a job. Instead He directed him to a coin waiting just for him in, of all places, a fish's mouth! Why didn't Jesus tell Peter to go get a job and meet back up with the team a month later? Because then Peter would have been just like everyone else—depending upon his own labor to provide for himself—and would have had to abandon his spiritual assignment.

There are always two different kingdoms in existence at any given time. The only difference is that they work in completely different manners. One kingdom is the one we all grew up with and have grown accustomed to. This is the earth-cursed kingdom. In this kingdom system, we will only have what we can run after and purchase by our own efforts. The other kingdom is the Kingdom of God system that allows us to have whatever we need just by learning how to access the Kingdom and following the direction of the Holy Spirit. In this Kingdom we don't have to be dependent upon our own abilities to run fast or labor tirelessly. This is relief the likes of which you can only experience through God's gift of provision.

The Kingdom Produces Every Time

Not long ago I was preaching in a friend's church. I had focused on First John 5:14-15, which says:

> *This is the confidence we have in approaching God: that if we ask anything according to His will, He hears us. And if we know that He hears us—whatever we ask—we know that we have what we asked of Him.*

My point was that we can always be confident in prayer and not just hope that what God has told us will come to pass.

When I finished, the pastor approached me, amazed at what I was preaching.

You see, I frequently use a lot of deer hunting stories when I teach because that is how God taught me about His Kingdom. I would hunt and freeze in the miserable cold and never get a deer. When I finally came to fully understand how God's Kingdom works, I would go out hunting and have my deer in the first 40 minutes—every time for the last 20 years!

My hunting illustrations caught the pastor's ear, and he began telling me of an upcoming moose hunting trip he was planning. He had gone year after year but had never got a moose. I then explained how he could know for certain that he would receive his moose. For sure, he would have to do his part, but he also had to believe that God would put that moose right in his scope. Before he left, I gave him and one of his hunting buddies a copy of my book *Faith Hunt*, which is a collection of faith-based hunting stories.

Of the five men who went on the hunting trip, it was these two who returned home with a trophy. Before they left, however, the pastor's son shared with his dad that he also wanted to bring home a moose. Because the son had become backslidden in his lifestyle, the pastor took the opportunity to pray with his son and share about the Kingdom of God. It wasn't long afterward that the son also took a moose. The guides on this trip said this was the most successful hunt they had ever had. Not surprisingly, the other two men on the trip didn't even see a moose while they were out.

Coincidence? Definitely not. Is it just chance that an airplane flies? No! The airplane flies because of laws that have been learned and written down so that anyone can use them once he or she understands them.

Seek First the Kingdom

In Matthew 6:31-33, Jesus was telling His followers to not worry but instead to seek the Kingdom and what God calls righteousness, or we could say what God considers right. When Jesus was saying to seek the Kingdom, He was saying to learn how the Kingdom operates and learn what God calls right. To define what God calls right we need to look at how God had originally made man to live—free from worry with every need he would ever have already provided by God Himself. Jesus is teaching us here that by learning how the Kingdom works and knowing it is God's will that we walk in life with everything we need (righteousness), we can walk free from worry and fear in life.

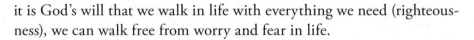

> *So do not worry, saying, "What shall we eat?" or "What shall we drink?" or "What shall we wear?" For the pagans run after all these things, and your heavenly Father knows that you need them.* ***But seek first His kingdom and His righteousness, and all these things will be given to you as well*** (Matthew 6:31-33).

It's our responsibility to take the time to seek and to learn how the Kingdom of God works. Once we understand this, we are able to access the provision the Father has for us. Based upon the statement in Matthew 6:24 about our inability to serve two masters at once, it then follows that if we're still running after money in our own strength, we will never be able to serve God. And if we can't serve God, the One who created us, we will never find out why we are here or our created purpose.

I told you at the opening of this final chapter that getting out of debt was the beginning, not the end. By learning how the Kingdom operates and by applying practical financial advice from the natural realm, you will be able to take the steps necessary to work your way out of debt. By winning in life and learning how to tap into the inheritance that is yours in the Kingdom of God, you are now free to follow God and realize your destiny—free from the shackles of debt and the weights of lack.

The practical financial principles I have given you in this book are powerful. By themselves, however, they are useless to help you truly win in life.

To truly win you must be able to discover your created purpose and, in that, you will find your destiny.

No, simply being out of debt does not constitute victory. Trust me, I've seen rich people who are not winning at the game of life. But there is absolutely nothing more fulfilling than uncovering your destiny and learning how the Kingdom of God works. Uncovering the secrets of the Kingdom of God is life changing.

As I tested these principles and found them to work, just as the Bible said they would (that should not have been a surprise), it became my mission to teach others.

A Business Is Turned Around

I want to let you read an email I received from a client in the spring of 2008. I think it will best illustrate how the Kingdom of God can change people's lives in the financial realm.

> *Gary, I want to wish you and your family a very blessed and prosperous 2008. I will say that your teaching has set me free as I will begin to explain. I was in corporate life and made a good salary and life was good. After the year 2000, I started my own business and did okay. I tithed and served God all during those years. About four years later, my business went south and I mean south. I ended up with huge credit card debt, almost had my house foreclosed on three times and just about lost everything. The only job I could get was to work at Fedex making $11/hr. and I took all sorts of odd jobs to just get by. I cleaned wash rooms, did handy man stuff, etc. As I began to ask around concerning why things were so bad, most of my friends said that God may be punishing me. I really began to question my life.*
>
> *There were times in my life when I woke up and cried because I wanted God to end it for me. I so wanted to drop dead. All was lost, or so I thought. Even at church they said, "Well, where is your God now? Look at what a mess your life is." Many would laugh at my downfall and many people who I thought were friends turned their backs on me.*
>
> *In January of 2007, I came across your tapes and listened to them over and over again. They set me so free. With excitement*

I turned my life over to God realizing that He was for me and not against me. I began to give to the Kingdom of God, out of my little $180 a week paycheck. I had been discouraged with God but your tapes told me that my money was not in heaven, and the only way God could get money to me was to show me where it was and then I would have to follow that direction. I realized then that I had missed it.

I could name quite a few opportunities that I had passed up because I was so discouraged. Now I saw the truth and I set out with courage. I began sowing from my weekly $180 pay check for a better job. I was able to get a contract job with a medical manufacturing company at $3,500 a week.

When the contract came to an end, I began to give more and thanked God for increase. I then secured a new contract for $5,500 a week in pay with a possibility of a new business on the horizon. The sky is the limit now. I have nothing but gratitude to the Father for what he has done in my life, and for bringing your teaching into my life and showing me how dangerous it is to have wrong thinking. With my wrong thinking and lack of faith, I was literally handing everything I owned over to the devil without a fight. I then sat there and thought it was God's desire for me to be broke.

I am not out of the woods yet, it is a process but this year I will be totally out of debt and I know that there is no end in sight for the good things the Lord has for me.[1]

I get these types of emails every day from people all around the world who have experienced the Kingdom of God for themselves, just like Drenda and I have. It's amazing how much people want to share their joy and their stories once they understand how the Kingdom of God works, how they can operate within it, and the tremendous changes in their lives as a result.

I trust that as you have read through this book you have been inspired to believe there are answers for your life. It is possible for you to "fix your money thing" and to find your God-given destiny—all at the same time! I know, because God helped me fix the money thing in my life when I was hopeless *and* had no future.

As I started to unravel the mysteries of the Kingdom, I began to discover my destiny as well. I trust that the plan presented in this book will give you a blueprint for your future, as well as help you find the money to carry it out. I also hope that the principles I've shared with you regarding the Kingdom of God and how it operates will change how you think and will encourage you to step out in faith.

For additional teaching concerning the Kingdom of God, go to my Website at FaithLifeNow.com. To contact my financial restructuring firm go to ForwardFinancialGroup.com. If we can be of service to you as you make this exciting journey, please contact us, we would love to hear your story.

appendix

sample plan to **financial freedom**

FORWARD
FINANCIAL GROUP

www.forwardfinancialgroup.com - 1.888.397.DEBT - P.O. Box 779 New Albany, OH 43054

> FIXING THE
money thing
FOR YOU.

PLAN TO FINANCIAL FREEDOM FOR:
Jim and Kathy Radcliff

Net Monthly Income:

Jim	$2,801.66
Kathy	$1,640.00

Total Net Income: $4,441.66

Tithes & Offerings	$650.00

Monthly Expenses:

House/Rent	$1,165.00
Auto Loan	$365.00
Auto Loan	$301.02

Total Loan Payments: $1,831.05

Credit Card Payments:

Visa	$175.00
Discover	$167.00
Sears	$96.00
Home Depot	$123.00

Total Credit Card Payments: $561.00

Insurance Payments:

Auto	$55.00
Homeowners	$31.00
Health	$265.00
Life	$102.00

Total Insurance Payments: $453.00

Living Expenses:

Food	$500.00
Telephone & Utilities	$231.00
Auto, gas, expenses	$110.00
Misc. newspaper, magazines, dues & gifts	$30.00
Entertainment	$50.00
Clothing	$100.00

Total Monthly Living Expenses: $1,021.00

Total Expenses: $4,441.66

Budget Deficit or Surplus: $0.00

RESTRUCTURING SUMMARY

THE RESULTS OF ASSET MANAGEMENT
TOTAL MONTHLY SAVINGS

Refinance	$252.83
Dropped Land Line (Telephone)	$26.00
Consolidation	$451.18
Taxes (Withholding Changes/Second Mortgage	$132.98
Tax Recovery (based on past 3 years)	$166.00
Cancel Credit Life Insurance	$35.00
Health Insurance Savings	$32.00
Free Checking	$8.00
Reduce Internet / Reduce Cable	$10.00
Removed PMI on Mortgage	$46.53
"Temporarily" stop 401(k)	$106.00
Auto and Home Insurance Survey	$12.00
Change Insurance Package	$54.04
Tax Planning	$92.00
Will / Pre-Paid Legal	($17.00)

Cash Reserve:

Cash Reserve Amount..$3,000.00

Built entirely with the $3,000.00 TAX RECOVERY lump sum and miscellaneous sales on eBay and Craig's List.

After the cash reserve is established, you begin accelerating the debt payoff.

Total Monthly Savings....................................$1,671.94

REAP THE BENEFITS

OF FINANCIAL RESTRUCTURING

Debt Elimination

Begin by applying the $1,671.94 to reduce your monthly debts starting with the highest interest rate loan. Each time a loan is paid off, that payment amount is added to the next loan to be accelerated.

First, Build the Cash Reserve:

Required Reserve...$3.000.00
Built entirely with $3,000 TAX RECOVERY Lump Sum

Next, the Auto #1:

Original Balance...$18,400.00
Interest Rate...7.00%
Normal Payment...$365.00
Balance at Acceleration...$18,400.00
Accelerated Payment...$2,036.94
The loan will be paid in month 10 after 10 accelerated payments.

Next, the 2nd Mortgage:

Original Balance...$23,500.80
Interest Rate...6.00%
Normal Payment...$260.91
Balance at Acceleration...$21,911.14
Accelerated Payment...$2,297.85
The loan will be paid in month 20 after 10 accelerated payments.

Total time required to build cash reserve and pay consumer debt:
20 months.

MORTGAGE ACCELERATION PROGRAM

1. Current Loan

A. Current Balance:	$157,500.00
B. Annual Interest Rate:	5.6%
C. Scheduled Number of Payments Remaining:	356
D. Monthly Payment:	$904.17
E. Balance at time of acceleration:	$153,874.08

2. Acceleration of Mortgage

A. Scheduled Monthly Payment:	$904.17
B. Monthly Acceleration Amount:	$2,297.85
C. Total Accelerated Monthly Payment:	$3,202.02
D. Time Required to Retire Debt:	54 Months
E. Total Time until you are DEBT FREE:	6.3 Years (76 months)

3. Amount of Interest Saved

A. Original Loan Payment Total:	$321,625.50
B. Accelerated Loan Payment Total	$188,941.01
C. Total Interest Saved on Mortgage	$132,684.49
D. Total Interest Saved (All Debt)	$138,733.23

Total Financial Freedom at Age 46

INVESTMENT PROGRAM

AGE AT START OF INVESTMENT: 46

Amount of investment per month: $3,202.02

Year	Age	Amount at 9%	Months
4	50	$196,036	48
8	54	$512,090	96
12	58	$1,021,641	144
16	62	$1,843,153	192
19	65	$2,775,058	228

Year	Age	Amount at 5%	Months
4	50	$169,754	48
8	54	$377,007	96
12	58	$630,041	144
16	62	$938,969	192
19	65	$1,214,675	228

CONCLUSION

BASED ON THE PRECEDING DATA, YOU COULD BE FREE FROM ALL DEBT IN 6.3 YEARS.

The plan assumes that your budget is sound and that you have a cash reserve set-up. (Please use the attached budget sheet for your records.) It also assumes that you are totally committed to being out of debt.

Based on your current income, you will avoid 4.2 years of slavery to lenders by following the plan. In a sense, it's like adding 4.2 years to your life. Think a minute about how good it will feel to be free from debt. You will be free to:

1. BE FREE TO FIND GOD'S PLAN FOR YOUR LIFE.

Now that you are not consumed every day with a survival mentality, you can find the real you and discover your destiny.

2. PROVIDE ADEQUATELY FOR YOUR FAMILY.

Being free financially provides freedom for you but also brings opportunities for your entire family to discover life in a whole new way.

3. BE FREE TO HELP OTHERS.

Everyone wants to leave a legacy and make a difference. Be free to reach out to loved ones or other people you care about. Give to a church, organization or charity. After all, it is not what we have but what we give away that really counts.

4. FUND YOUR PASSION AND LIFE GOALS.

Money is simply a tool, but a tool is invaluable when you are building a house. So it is with money. Forward Financial Group believes that everyone has an assignment, and they were created with a purpose in mind. Being free financially allows your money to be the tool you need, when you need it.

endnotes

Chapter 2

1. Jackson Lears, "The American Way of Debt," *The New York Times*. June 11, 2006. http://www.nytimes.com/2006/06/11/magazine/11wwln_lede.html?pagewanted=all.

2. John Hartgen, "Total U.S. Bankruptcies Up," American Bankruptcy Institute. Nov. 4, 2009. http://www.abiworld.org/AM/Template.cfm?Section=Home&TEMPLATE=/CM/ContentDisplay.cfm&CONTENTID=58407.

3. "Stop Trying to Keep Up with the Jones," MoneyMatters101.com. http://moneymatters101.com/debt/thejones.asp.

4. Juliet Schor, *The Overspent American* (New York: 1st HarperPerennial edition; April 7, 1999), 75.

5. Survey: "Most Americans fail the emergency-fund test," Bankrate.com. http://www.bankrate.com/brm/news/sav/20060621a1.asp.

6. Schor, 75.

7. Credit Card Nation, "History of Consumer Spending As % of Disposable Income 1929 through 2007." April 1, 2009. http://www.freeby50.com/2009/04/history-of-consumer-spending-as-of.html.

8. Robert Manning, "Evolution of the Credit Card," Oct. 2009. www.creditcardnation.com/pdfs/Evolution_of_Credit_Cards.pdf.

9. Money-Zine.com, "Credit Card and Debt Statistics," 2009. www.money-zine.com/Financial-Planning/Debt-Consolidation/Credit-Card-Debt-Statistics/.

10. Martin Vaughan, "Congress Hammers Out Breaks for Homeowners" *The Wall Street Journal*, April 23, 2008.

11. Kevin Chiu, Housing Predictor, "Bank Foreclosures Set New Record High" May 13, 2010. http://www.housingpredictor.com/record-high-foreclosures.html.

12. "Facts About How People Handle Money" Free Money Finance, June 21, 2007. http://www.freemoneyfinance.com/2007/06/facts_about_how.html.

13. Kim Khan, "How Does Your Debt Compare," http://moneycentral.msn.com/content/SavingandDebt/P70741.asp?Printer.

14. Edward Tonini, Alliance Credit Counseling, "Spending Plan Development," http://knowdebt.org/spending-plan-development.

15. Moneyrelationship.com, "The Average Net Worth of Americans: Where Do You Stand," March 16, 2009. http://www.moneyrelationship.com/retirement/the-average-net-worth-of-americans-where-do-you-stand/.

16. Tracy Turner, "Debt Is People's Biggest Worry...Finance Problems Rank Higher Than Terrorism and Disasters," *The Columbus Dispatch* (July 19, 2006).

17. Kathy Chu, "Many Marriages Today Are 'Til Debt Do Us Part,'" *USA Today* (April 28, 2006).

18. Personal email to author; name withheld for confidentiality.

19. Kathy Chu, "Retirees Up Against Debt," *USA Today* (January 23, 2007).

Chapter 3

1. Michael Abramowitz, "Department Store Credit Cards," www.bankrate.com/brm/news/advice/19990824c/asp.
2. Peter Davidson, "Top 10 Hidden Dangers of Credit Cards," www.bankrate.com/brm/news/debt/20040915a1.asp.
3. www.crown.org/tools/calculators/CreditCard_MinimumPayment.aspx.
4. Lucy Lazarony, "Credit Cards Teaching Students a Costly Lesson," http://bankrate.com/brm/news/cc/9980605.asp.
5. Ken Bensinger, "Surviving Debt," www.smartmoney.com./mag/index.cfm?story=august2007-debt.
6. Jessica Bennet, "American Debt: Escaping the Credit-Card Quagmire," http://www.msnbc.msn.com/id/14366431/site/newsweek.
7. http://www.spendonlife.com/content/CreditCardDebtElimination-AndFactsAboutDebtInAmerica-1-223-3.ashx.
8. Ibid.
9. www.house.gov/apps/list/hearing/financialsucs_dem/htw.lmarth042607.pdf.
10. Center for Responsible Lending, "Driving Borrowers to Financial Ruin," Jan. 1, 2001. http://www.responsiblelending.org/issues/cartitle/?log-event+sp2f-view-item&nid=341664.
11. Andy Vuong, "Colorado lawmakers look to close payday loan loophole," *The Denver Post*, Sept. 25, 2005.
12. Center for Responsible Lending, "Driving Borrowers to Financial Ruin," Jan. 1, 2001. http://www.responsiblelending.org/payday-lending/.
13. Ibid.
14. Jean Ann Fox, "The Basics: 5 Dangerous Loans to Leave Alone," http://www.moneycentral.msn.com/content/banking/betterbanking/P117581.asp.

15. Ellen Schloemer, Wei Li, Keith Ernst, Kathleen Keest, "Executive Summary—Losing Ground: Foreclosures in the Subprime Market and Their Cost to Homeowners" (December 2006), 2.

Chapter 4

1. Don McAlvany, *The McAlvany Intelligence Advisor,* Dec. 2006.
2. Tula Connell, "July Job Numbers: Still a Crisis," AFL-CIO, Aug. 6, 2010. http://blog.aflcio.org/2010/08/06/131000-jobs-lost-in-july/.
3. Don McAlvany, The *McAlvany Intelligence Advisor*, Aug. 2008.
4. Don McAlvany, *McAlvany Intelligence Advisor*, Jan 2010.
5. "The National Debt Clock," *www.defeatthedebt.com.*
6. Conference attended by author, May, 2010.
7. Harry Figgie, *Bankrupcy 1995: The Coming Collapse of America and How to Stop It* (Boston: Little, Brown and Co, 1993).
8. "The National Debt Clock," *www.defeatthedebt.com.*
9. Paul Toscano, CNBC, "Countries Overloaded By Debt," Oct. 28, 2009. http://www.cnbc.com/id/33506526.
10. Don McAlvany, *McAlvany Intelligence Advisor,* Jan. 2010.
11. Ken Besinger, "Surviving Debt," *Smart Money Magazine,* Aug. 8, 2007. http://www.smartmoney.com/personal-finance/debt/surviving-debt-21652/.
12. Catherine Clifford, "Befuddled By Debt? You're Not Alone," Feb. 26, 2008. http://money.cnn.com/2008/02/26/pf/financial_illiteracy/index.htm.
13. Don McAlvany, *McAlvany Intelligence Advisor*, Jan 2010.
14. Michael R. Crittenden, "FDIC Sees More Failures as Problem Banks Hit 775" *The Wall Street Journal*. May 21, 2010 .
15. Don McAlvany, *McAlvany Intelligence Advisor*, April 2004.

16. Edward Niedermeyer, "Bailout Watch 573," Nov. 19, 2009. http://www.thetruthaboutcars.com/bailout-watch-573-gm-bailout-cost-taxpayers-12200-per-car/.

17. Scott Patterson and Tom Lauricella, "Did a Big Bet Help Trigger 'Black Swan' Stock Swoon?" *The Wall Street Journal,* Tues. May 10, 2010.

18. "Employment Situation Summary" http://www.bls.gov/news.release/empsit.nr0.htm.

19. Christian Weller, "Drowning In Debt," www.americanprogress.org/issues/2006.

20. Ibid.

21. Warren Graham, *Perfect Storm*, www.bestsyndication.com, 9/10/06. Mark Zandi, "Mortgage Plan Too Late," www.freedomworks.org/newsroom/media-template.php?issue_id=3752.

22. Steve Slavin, *USA Today.*

23. Mike Whitney, "Day of Reckoning," www.informationclearinghouse.info/ariticle14905htm.

24. David Walker, "Financial Tsunami," www.news.bbc.co.uk/2/hi/programmes/hardtalk/4857646.st.

25. Ibid.

26. James Turk, *The Daily Reckoning*, www.dailyreckoning.com/issues/2007/DR021307.html.

27. Ibid.

28. www.aflcio.org/aboutus/.../publications/magazine/0404_manufacturing.cfm.

29. www.aflcio.org/issues/jobseconomy/jobs/outsourcing_problems.cfm.

30. Matt Krantz, "Hopes Stocks Had Bottomed Are Fading Fast," *USA Today*, June 28, 2008.

31. Norihiko Shirouzu, "Cruising Into China's Booming Car Market," *Wall Street Journal*, April 29, 2010.

32. Don McAlvany, *McAlvany Intelligence Advisor*, April, 2007.

33. Elizabeth Williamson, "Will Nickel-Free Nickels Make a Dime's Worth of Difference?" *Wall Street Journal*, April 24, 2010.

34. Lawrence H. Officer and Samuel H. Williamson, "Purchasing Power of Money in the United States from 1774 to 2010," *MeasuringWorth*, 2009. http://www.measuringworth.com/ppowerus/.

Chapter 11

1. Crown Financial Ministries. www.Crown.org.

Chapter 12

1. Venita Van Caspel, *Life Insurance: The Great National Consumer Dilemma* (New York: Simon and Schuster, New York, 1983).

Chapter 13

1. Congressional record, July 18th, 2001, page 13631.

2. *Money* Magazine. 3/1987-97.

3. Ibid.

4. Ibid.

5. Ibid.

6. Kevin McCormally, *Cut Your Taxes* (New York: Kiplinger/Times Business Books, 1997).

7. John Waggoner, "Savvy Strategies for Tax Refunds," *USA Today,* March 23, 2006.

Chapter 14

1. Audit My Bills, Inc. Columbus, OH auditmybills.com.

2. Ibid.

3. Ibid.

4. Ibid.

5. Ibid.

6. *The Columbus Dispatch*, July 11, 2003.

7. Theo Francis and Mark H. Anderson, "Ruling Allows Workers to Sue on 401k Losses," *Wall Street Journal,* Feb. 21, 2008. online.wsj.com/article/NA_WSJ_PUB:SB120355797559081769.html.

Chapter 15

1. Joe Light, "7 Ways to Fight Property Taxes," *Money Magazine*, Feb. 13, 2008.

2. *The Columbus Dispatch.*

3. www.Allstate.com.

4. Alan Buerger, www.coventry.com.

5. "Unclaimed Aid in Ohio: $1.5 Billion a Year." *The Columbus Dispatch,* April 29, 2007.

Chapter 16

1. Robertson Education Empowerment Foundation (REEF), "The Biggest Gamble of Your Life (Is College Worth It?)" www.aboutreef.org/is-college-worth-it.html.

2. Ibid.

3. Ibid.

4. 10/earlyshow/contributors/raymartin/main2785428.shtml.

5. Ibid.

6. Warren Jaeger, *How to Plan, Subcontract, and Build Your Dream House and Save $50,000* (LaGrangeville, NY: Trojan Homes, NY: January, 1998).

7. Bryant Clark, *How to Build Your Dream House with No Experience and Save $60,000.*, self-published.

Chapter 18

1. Jack Marrion, *Index Annuities*; *Power and Protection* (St. Louis: Advantage Compendium, 2004), 27-28.

2. Thomas Brueckner, www.seniorfo.com.

3. John Bogle, "The Emperor's New Mutual Funds," *The Wall Street Journal* (July 8, 2005).

4. Ibid.

5. Karlan Tucker, Tucker Advisory Group, www.Tuckeradvisorygroup.com.

Chapter 19

1. Personal email to author, name and date withheld for confidentiality.

Gary Keesee

Biography

A few years after their wedding, Gary and Drenda found themselves with a mountain of debt and nowhere to turn. Desperate for real answers to life's toughest questions concerning faith, family, and finances, the Keesees began to get serious about the Bible. It was there they found hope, and through applying sound financial principles, their lives truly changed from the inside out. They paid off all of their debt, made a stronger commitment to their marriage, and rebuilt their financial business, catering it toward helping families live financially free.

Gary and Drenda's strong desire to minister in the marketplace fueled the creation of their many businesses, which are centered around helping people with their finances. Forward Financial Group alone has helped hundreds of thousands of clients, and Gary continues to encourage Christians to go out into the business world and make a difference.

Faith Life Now, founded by Gary and Drenda, offers worldwide conferences, weekly television programming, books and other resources, practical financial support, and personalized help for people who need answers. The Keesees are passionate about getting down to the basics of how to live a different kind of life, and they love to share their stories.

Gary holds a B.A. from Oral Roberts University. Gary and Drenda have raised five godly children, Amy, Timothy, Thomas, PollyAnne and Kirsten, all of whom serve in the ministry along with their spouses. The Keesees reside in Columbus, OH.

www.garykeesee.com

www.faithlifechurch.org